CAMBRIDGE IGCSE® ECONOMICS

Revision Guide

Andrew Gillespie

Contents

Chapter 3 Microeconomic decision makers

Chapter 5 Economic development

Chapter 6 International trade and globalisation

Introduction

This revision guide will help you to revise and practise the skills and knowledge required by the Cambridge IGCSE and O Level Economics syllabuses. It covers all of the learning objectives in the Economics syllabuses.

The guide is divided into six chapters. Each chapter covers one of the topics in the syllabuses.

The syllabuses contain a lot of subject specific vocabulary that you need to learn. Key words are highlighted in bold in the main text and the definitions are summarised in the Glossary at the end of the book.

You will find Revision tips on many of the pages in the guide. They explain how to avoid some common errors that students make when they write answers to questions.

Revision is only successful if you do something active, rather than simply reading. You could try rewriting some of the material in a different form. For example, you could convert a paragraph of text into a series of bullet points, or change a set of bullet points into a table.

There are Quick test questions at the end of each sub-topic. Use these to check that you have understood and remembered the content you have just worked through. The answers to these questions are at the back of the book.

At the end of each chapter, there is a set of Exam-style practice questions. These are designed to help you prepare for the theory parts of your examinations. Each question has a mark allocation, which you should use to help you decide how much to write and how much detail to give in your answer. The questions, example answers, marks awarded and comments that appear in the book were written by the author. Note that in examinations, the way marks would be awarded to answers like these may be different.

You will find a list of the contents on pages 2 to 6. You could use this to keep track of your progress as you work through the guide – tick the box in one colour when you have first worked through a section and then in another colour when you have gone over it again and answered all of the questions correctly.

The nature of the economic problem

Finite resources and unlimited wants

The resources of an economy are inputs into the production process. They are:

- **land**
- **labour**
- **capital**
- **enterprise**.

Most **resources** are finite – once they have been used, they cannot be replaced.

Renewable resources are commodities that are replaceable, such as solar energy, fish stocks or forestry. They can be sustained over time, providing the rate of extraction is less than or equal to the rate of renewal.

At any moment in time, resources are fixed in terms of their quantity and quality, which means there is a limit to what can be produced. This affects all the **economic agents** (different groups in the economy):

- **consumers** – have limited **income** and must decide how to use it
- **employees** (workers) – have limited time and must decide how to use it
- **producers** – have limited funds and must decide what to do with them, e.g. whether to invest in new machinery or new office space
- **government** – have limited funds and must decide what to do with them, e.g. whether to invest in education or healthcare.

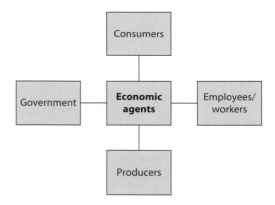

Finite resources limit what can be produced. However, human wants (what we would like) and needs (what we must have, e.g. water and food) are unlimited. This means resources are scarce and choices have to be made about what to do with them.

> **Revision tip**
>
> When answering a question, remember to think about the effect of any change on the different economic agents: consumers, employees, producers and government. A given policy may be good for some agents but not for others.

Finite resources and unlimited wants lead to scarcity and choice. The **basic economic problem** is that decisions have to be made about the choice and allocation of resources to determine:

- what is produced
- how it is produced
- who products are produced for.

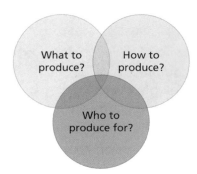

Economic and free goods

The provision of **economic goods** involves an **opportunity cost** – to produce the good, resources have to be moved from the production of another good. For example, to produce more laptops, employees may be moved from producing PCs. We have more of one product, but have sacrificed something in return.

The opportunity cost of any decision is measured in terms of what has been sacrificed in the next best alternative.

The provision of a **free good** does not involve an opportunity cost. Air is a free good – it exists and, in general, does not require other goods to be sacrificed to have more of it.

Revision tip

Sometimes free goods become economic goods. For example, if air becomes polluted and has to be cleaned up, this process involves resources and has an opportunity cost.

Quick test

1. Explain the difference between an economic good and a free good.
2. Explain what is meant by a 'finite resource'.
3. State **three** economic agents.
4. Explain what is meant by 'the basic economic problem'.
5. Explain what is meant by a 'renewable resource'.

Factors of production

Factors of production and their rewards

The **factors of production** in an economy are used in the production process to produce goods and services. They are:

- **land** – including natural resources such as oil
- **labour** – the number and skills of the workforce
- **capital** – the quality and quantity of machinery and equipment
- **enterprise** – the management expertise needed to think of new products and processes and combine resources to set up a new project or business.

The people who come up with new ideas and take the risk to develop new business opportunities are called **entrepreneurs**.

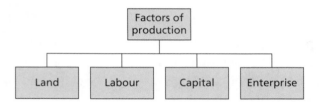

The rewards for the factors of production are:

- wages for employees
- rent for land
- interest earned on capital
- **profit** for enterprise.

Mobility of the factors of production

Factor mobility refers to how easily factors can move from one business or industry to another. Immobility means it is difficult for resources to be reallocated.

Labour immobility may occur due to:

- **occupational immobility**, when there are differences in the skills needed, e.g. a plumber cannot easily become a doctor; it would take several years to retrain
- **geographical immobility**, when it is difficult to move to another area, e.g. high house prices in a particular region may make it difficult for people from other regions to relocate there.

Quantity and quality of the factors of production

The amount of output that can be produced with the factors of production depends on their quality and quality. For example:

- the more people there are in the workforce, and the better their training and skills, the more productive it can be
- machinery that uses the latest technology may be more productive than older machinery.

> You must be able to:
> - explain what is meant by 'factors of production'
> - explain what is meant by the 'mobility' and 'immobility' of factors of production
> - explain why the quantity and quality factors of production may change over time.

Revision tip

The word 'capital' can be confusing as it has different meanings. It can mean 'capital goods', such as machines or equipment. However, money is often referred to as 'capital' too.

Revision tip

Remember, resources are fixed in terms of quantity and quality at any moment, but can change over time.

Changes in factors of production can occur over time. For example:

- investment in technology and equipment can improve the quantity and quality of capital
- better training and education or more apprenticeships can improve the quality of the workforce
- a growth in the **population** size, e.g. more people coming into a country than leaving it (net migration), can increase the number of the workforce
- the use of better technology, e.g. use of fertilisers on farmland or better technology to access shale gas, can improve the **productivity** of the land.

Quick test

1. What is meant by 'enterprise'?
2. Give **three** factors of production.
3. Explain how the quantity of capital may be improved over time.
4. Explain what is meant by 'labour immobility'.
5. Explain how the quality of labour may be improved over time.
6. What is an 'entrepreneur'?

Opportunity cost and the production possibility curve diagram (PPC)

Opportunity cost and its influence on decision-making

Opportunity cost refers to what is sacrificed in the next best alternative when a decision is made. For example, if resources are put into the provision of more schools, the opportunity cost may be fewer hospitals.

Given the fact that there are limited resources at any given moment, it is impossible to have more of everything – something has to be sacrificed to have more of one product, i.e. there is an opportunity cost.

When making any decision, the decision maker should consider what else could be done with the resources, i.e. what is the opportunity cost? This is known as the real cost of an economic decision (as opposed to its financial cost).

The production possibility curve diagram (PPC)

The **production possibility curve (PPC)** shows the maximum goods and services that can be produced given the existing resources and technology.

If the economy is producing on the PPC, it is **productively efficient** – more of one product can only be produced if less of another is produced. There is an opportunity cost.

For example, in the diagram below, if resources are moved out of Product A and into Product B, the economy may move from Y to Z. The opportunity cost of the extra XZ units of B is the YX units of A.

If the economy is producing inside the PPC (e.g. at X), it is **productively inefficient** – more of one product could be produced without producing less of another. This is because resources are being used inefficiently or the economy is not working at full capacity, e.g. there is unemployment.

Productive inefficiency

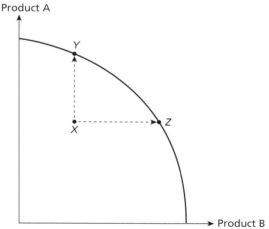

You must be able to:
- explain what is meant by 'opportunity cost'
- explain the significance of opportunity cost
- understand the meaning of the production possibility curve (PPC)
- show the concept of opportunity cost on a production possibility curve.

> **Revision tip**
>
> Remember that any policy decision will involve an opportunity cost. This should be considered before deciding whether to go ahead with the policy.

> **Revision tip**
>
> When drawing the PPC, remember to label the axes 'Product A' and 'Product B'.

Over time, the PPC can shift outwards if there is an improvement in the quality and quantity of resources. This shows **economic growth**.

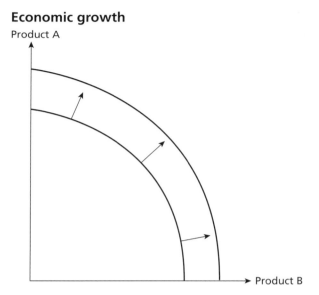

Economic growth

Revision tip

The PPC is an important concept in economics. Make sure you can use it to show a reallocation of resources between industries, a growth in the economy and economic inefficiency.

Trade

A country cannot produce outside of its PPC given its existing resources. However, if it trades some of its goods abroad, it is possible for a country to consume outside the PPC. If a country **specialises** in producing Product A, it may be able to trade some of Product A abroad in return for higher levels of Product B than it could produce itself. If countries specialise in producing goods and services that they are particularly good at and then trade them with others who are particularly good at something else, they can all benefit.

Capital goods versus consumption goods

Capital goods, such as machines, are an investment for the future. **Consumption goods**, such as food, are consumed now. If an economy puts most if its resources into capital goods, it may lead to greater output and economic growth in the future. If the economy produces mainly consumption goods, it means there is little investment in the future and economic growth is likely to be lower.

Quick test

1. Explain what is meant by 'opportunity cost'.
2. Explain what is shown by the production possibility curve (PPC).
3. Explain how opportunity cost can be shown on a PPC.
4. Explain why operating on the PPC is productively efficient.
5. Explain why the PPC may move outwards over time.

Exam-style practice questions

1 What is meant by 'the basic economic problem'? [1]

   a) abundance and choice

   b) abundance and freedom

   c) scarcity and choice

   d) scarcity and freedom

2 A business invests in a new factory. Which factor of production has increased? [1]

   a) capital

   b) enterprise

   c) labour

   d) land

3 Opportunity cost refers to the sacrifice of what? [1]

   a) a more modern alternative

   b) the lowest cost alternative

   c) the most different alternative

   d) the next best alternative

4 How does a production possibility curve (PPC) show that scarcity exists? [1]

   a) It shows that as demand increases for a product, its price rises.

   b) It shows that as more resources are used to produce a product, its price rises.

   c) It shows that at any point outside the PPC, an economy is wasting resources.

   d) It shows that there is a limit to the quantity of products that can be produced with existing resources and technology.

5 An economy is producing efficiently and shifts resources from producing food to computers. Which could describe the movement? [1]

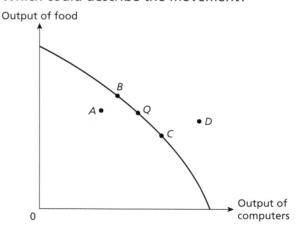

   a) AB

   b) BQ

   c) CQ

   d) CD

6 Why are wants **not** fully satisfied in an economy? [1]

a) An economy can only produce a limited amount of goods and services.

b) Governments cannot print enough money to pay for goods and services.

c) There is an over-production of goods and services by business organisations.

d) Workers are too skilled for the requirements of the jobs available.

7 **South Korea's balance of trade**

Fig. 1: South Korea's GDP (income), 1960–2016

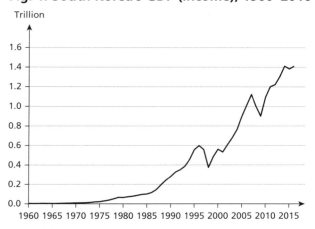

Fig. 2: South Korea's population, 1960–2016

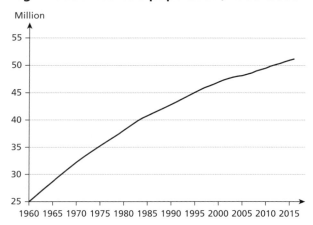

Fig. 3: South Korea's balance of trade, 2012–2016

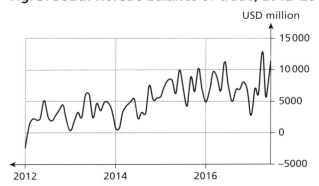

The balance of trade measures the difference between a country's export revenue from goods and services and import spending over a given period.

South Korea is a modern economic miracle. Over the last forty years it has experienced rapid economic growth and has become a high-technology industrialised economy. By comparison, the economy of its neighbour, North Korea, remains very much based on the primary sector (farming and extractive industries) and the income per person is low.

Much of South Korea's progress is due to the government, which encouraged investment in capital, education and training. As a result, the country has a well-equipped and highly-qualified workforce.

The South Korean government appreciated the importance of trade for the future of the economy. It encouraged the import of raw materials and components rather than consumer goods in order to help businesses grow. It also gave incentives for saving and for the production of capital goods, rather than encouraging money to be spent on consumption. These savings provided funds for investment.

South Korea now has well-developed secondary (manufacturing) and tertiary (service) sectors.

a) Calculate the percentage increase in population in South Korea between 2015 and 1960. **[2]**

b) Explain what is meant by the primary sector. **[2]**

c) Explain what is meant by 'rapid economic growth' in South Korea. **[2]**

d) Show the economic growth of South Korea using a production possibility curve (PPC) diagram. **[4]**

e) Explain how investment in capital by South Korean businesses can encourage economic growth. **[4]**

f) Analyse how greater trade by South Korea can help lead to consumption outside the PPC of the economy. **[4]**

g) South Korea has invested heavily in education. Discuss whether investing in education is a good way to help an economy grow. **[6]**

h) South Korea has encouraged the production of capital goods. Discuss whether it is better for economies to produce capital goods or goods for consumption. **[6]**

8 Nigeria's spending on education is low compared to most other countries. In 2017, the Nigerian National Assembly allocated 6.4% of its total budget. By comparison, 31% of Ghana's annual budget goes to education, followed by Cote d'Ivoire which allocates 22% of its annual budget to education. Many students from Nigeria go abroad to study. This education abroad has an opportunity cost for consumers and for all economic agents in the country, especially when most students do not return home after their studies.

a) Define opportunity cost. **[2]**

b) Explain how the production possibility curve (PPC) can show the concept of opportunity cost. Use a diagram in your answer. **[4]**

c) Analyse the possible effect of low investment in education on the growth of an economy. **[6]**

d) Discuss the extent to which the concept of opportunity cost is only of use to consumers. **[8]**

9 China has a high supply of some factors of production. For many years the solution to the basic economic problem in China came through a command (planned) economy. The government introduced reforms to become more of a free market in 1978. Since then, GDP growth has averaged nearly 10 per cent a year and has lifted more than 800 million people out of poverty.

a) Identify factors of production in an economy. **[2]**

b) Explain what is meant by 'the basic economic problem'. **[4]**

c) Analyse the possible causes of economic growth. **[6]**

d) Discuss whether the free market is a better way to allocate resources than a command economy. **[8]**

Micro and macroeconomics

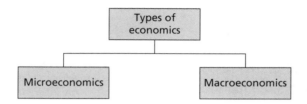

Types of economics
Microeconomics
Macroeconomics

Microeconomics

Microeconomics refers to the allocation of resources within specific **markets**, i.e. the market for a particular good or service.

Microeconomics may consider factors such as:

• the price of oil
• house prices in an area
• the wages of a particular type of worker.

Macroeconomics

Macroeconomics refers to the allocation of resources within the economy as a whole.

Macroeconomics involves factors such as:

• unemployment
• trade flows
• price levels in an economy.

 Revision tip

Microeconomics and macroeconomics are related. The whole economy (macro) is made up of many different individual markets (micro).

Quick test

1. What is meant by 'microeconomics'?
2. What is meant by 'macroeconomics'?
3. Analysing changes in the growth of the economy is part of macroeconomics. True or false?
4. Analysing changes in property prices in the capital of a country is part of macroeconomics. True or false?
5. Analysing changes in the unemployment levels in a country is part of microeconomics. True or false?

The role of markets in allocating resources

The market system

Markets are made up of demand and supply. They have buyers and sellers.

The price adjusts in a market to bring about **equilibrium** between supply and demand, i.e. a point where the quantity supplied equals the quantity demanded.

There are prices in many different markets within an economy, e.g. the price of a car, the price of a house, the price of a currency or the price of labour.

Introduction to the price mechanism

Equilibrium occurs when, at the given price, the quantity supplied equals the quantity demanded.

Disequilibrium occurs when, at the given price:
- the quantity demanded is greater than the quantity supplied (there is a **shortage**)

OR
- the quantity supplied is greater than the quantity demanded (there is a **surplus**).

The **price mechanism** is the process whereby the price adjusts to bring about equilibrium in a market. The price acts as:
- an incentive to producers to produce more or less
- a signal to other producers to enter or exit the industry
- a rationing device – it affects the quantity demanded.

For example, if there is too much demand in a market, the price will rise. This will:
- act as an incentive for existing producers to produce more
- encourage other producers to enter the market
- reduce the quantity demanded.

The price will continue to rise until equilibrium was restored.

Equilibrium is a position of stability in a market – there is no incentive to change at the given price and existing supply and demand conditions.

If the price in a market increases or decreases, it will be due to a shift in demand or supply. The shift will create excess demand or excess supply and the price will adjust, changing the quantity demanded and quantity supplied until a new equilibrium is reached.

> You must be able to:
> - explain what is meant by 'a market' and the 'market system'
> - explain the role of the price mechanism
> - explain what is meant by 'equilibrium'.

> ### Revision tip
>
> It is important to remember that economic diagrams, such as supply curves and demand curves, assume that all other factors are unchanged.

> ### Revision tip
>
> It is important to identify the cause of a change in the equilibrium price or quantity, e.g. was it a shift in demand or a shift in supply?

Quick test

1. Explain what is shown by a supply curve.
2. Explain what is shown by a demand curve.
3. Explain what is meant by 'equilibrium' in a market.
4. What is the role of the price mechanism?
5. What causes price changes in markets?

Demand

Demand

A **demand curve** shows the quantity that consumers are willing and able to buy at each and every price, all other factors unchanged.

Other influences on demand, apart from price, include:

- the prices of other goods and services
- income levels
- the marketing activities of the business
- the size of the buying population.

Price and demand

A **movement along a demand curve** leads to a change in the quantity demanded:

- a **contraction** of demand occurs when the price rises and there is a decrease in the quantity demanded
- an **extension** of demand occurs when the price falls and there is an increase in the quantity demanded.

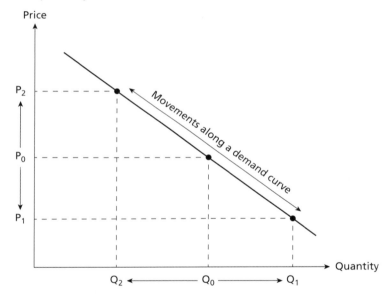

Conditions of demand

A **shift in demand** occurs due to a change in factors other than price, e.g. income, advertising, the price of other products or the number of consumers. When these change, there is a change in the quantity demanded at each and every price and the demand curve shifts.

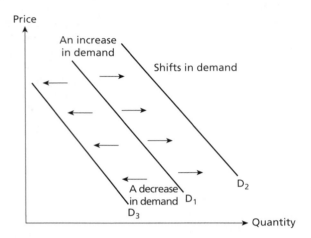

An outward shift (an increase) in demand can be caused by:

- more effective marketing, e.g. better advertising and greater brand loyalty
- an increase in income – for **normal goods** or services, more is demanded when income increases (note that for inferior goods or services, when income increases, less is demanded at each and every price, e.g. with more income, people may switch from using buses to buying and using their own car)
- an increase in the price of a **substitute** – consumers may switch from a substitute product (similar competitor product), which has become relatively expensive, to this product
- a decrease in the price of a **complement**, e.g. computer printers and printer cartridges are complements (the consumer needs both) so, if the price of the printer cartridges decreases, demand for the printer may increase (products that are brought together are in **joint demand**).

An inward shift (a decrease) in demand can be cause by:

- a reduction in marketing activities – with less promotion, the quantity demanded may fall
- a decrease in income – for normal goods and services, less is demanded when income decreases (note that for inferior goods and services, when income decreases, more is demanded at each and every price, i.e. customers switch back to the inferior products)
- a decrease in the price of a substitute – this will increase the quantity demanded of the substitute and reduce the quantity demanded of this product
- an increase in the price of a complement – this will cause less demand for the complement and for the product itself
- a decrease in the market size – a fall in the number of buyers will reduce demand.

Individual and market demand

An **individual demand curve** shows the quantity an individual consumer is willing and able to buy at each price, all other factors unchanged.

The **market demand curve**, for the market as a whole (i.e. for all consumers), is constructed by adding together the quantity demanded by all the different consumers at each and every price, all other factors unchanged. It is the horizontal summation of the individual demand curves.

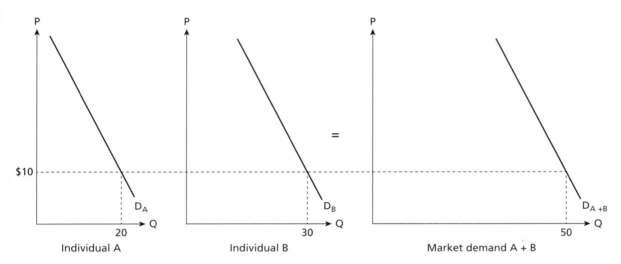

Individual A   Individual B   Market demand A + B

Quick test

1. What assumption is made when drawing a demand curve?

2. Give **one** reason why a demand curve for a product may shift outwards.

3. Give **one** reason why a demand curve for a product may shift inwards.

4. Explain the difference between a movement along a demand curve and a shift in demand.

5. Explain the difference between individual and market demand curves.

Supply

Supply

A **supply curve** shows the quantity that producers are willing and able to produce at each and every price, all other factors unchanged.

The amount that can be supplied at any price depends on factors such as:

- the number of producers
- the costs of resources, such as materials and labour
- the state of technology
- the way in which work is organised and managed
- taxes on producers or subsidies for producers.

Price and supply

A **movement along a supply curve** occurs when the price changes:

- an **extension** in supply is due to a rise in price, which increases the quantity supplied
- a **contraction** in supply is due to a fall in price, which reduces the quantity supplied.

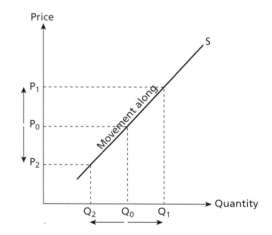

Conditions of supply

A **shift in supply** means more or less is supplied at each and every price.

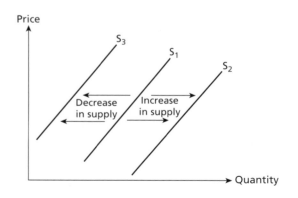

You must be able to:
- explain what is shown by a supply curve
- explain the difference between a movement along the curve and a shift in supply
- explain what can cause the supply curve to shift
- explain the difference between an individual and market supply curve.

> **Revision tip**
>
> Make sure you clearly understand the difference between a movement along a supply curve and a shift in supply.

Increase in supply (outward shift)	Decrease in supply (inward shift)
more producers	fewer producers
lower costs, e.g. lower wages or more subsidies	higher costs, e.g. higher wages or **indirect taxes**
better technology / working methods	poorer working methods
more capital equipment	less capital equipment

Individual and market supply

An **individual supply curve** shows the quantity an individual producer is willing and able to produce at each price and every price, all other factors unchanged.

The **market supply curve**, for the market as a whole (i.e. for all producers), is constructed by adding together the quantity supplied by all the different producers at each price and every price. It is the horizontal summation of the individual supply curves.

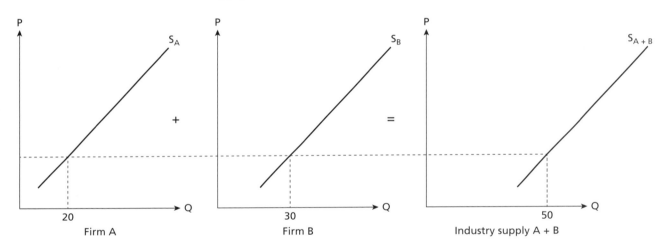

Firm A + Firm B = Industry supply A + B

Quick test

1. What assumption is made when drawing a supply curve?
2. Give **one** reason why a supply curve for a product may shift outwards.
3. Explain **one** reason why a supply curve for a product may shift inwards.
4. Explain the difference between a movement along a supply curve and a shift in supply.
5. Explain the difference between individual and market supply curves.

Price determination

Markets

The demand curve for a product is assumed to be downward sloping – at lower prices, the quantity demanded is greater.

The supply curve is assumed to be upward sloping – at higher prices, the quantity producers are willing and able to produce increases.

A shortage

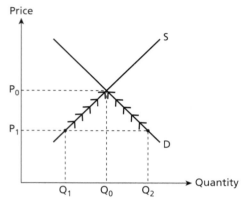

A **shortage** occurs if the quantity demanded (Q_2) is greater than the quantity supplied (Q_1), e.g. at P1. The price will increase, which reduces the quantity demanded and increases the quantity supplied until equilibrium is reached at P_0Q_0.

A surplus

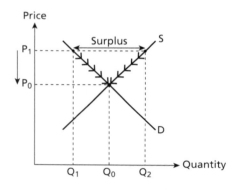

A **surplus** occurs when, at the given price, the quantity supplied (Q_2) is greater than the quantity demanded (Q_1). The price will fall, which reduces the quantity supplied and increases the quantity demanded until equilibrium is reached at P_0Q_0.

> You must be able to:
> - explain the meaning of 'a shortage'
> - explain the meaning of 'a surplus'
> - explain the meaning of market equilibrium and disequilibrium
> - use supply and demand diagrams to identify equilibrium and disequilibrium prices.

Market equilibrium and disequilibrium

Market **equilibrium** occurs at the price where quantity supplied equals quantity demanded and there is no incentive to change.

Disequilibrium occurs when, at the given price, the quantity demanded is greater than the quantity supplied (there is a shortage) or the quantity supplied is greater than the quantity demanded (excess supply).

Revision tip

Make sure you can differentiate between the cause and the effect of a change. An increase in demand may lead to a higher equilibrium price in a market. A higher price does not lead to an increase in demand.

Quick test

1. What is meant by 'market equilibrium'?
2. What is it called if, at a given price, the quantity demanded is greater than the quantity supplied?
3. What is it called if, at a given price, the quantity demanded is less than the quantity supplied?
4. If the quantity demanded is greater than the quantity supplied at a given price, is the price likely to increase or decrease?
5. What is meant by 'market disequilibrium'?

Price changes

Changes in supply and demand conditions

An increase in demand

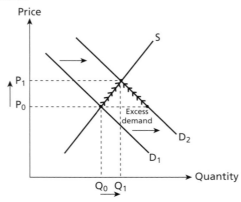

The market is initially at equilibrium at P_0Q_0. Demand increases and shifts outwards. At the existing price, there is now excess demand. The price increases, which reduces the quantity demanded and increases the quantity supplied until a new equilibrium price and quantity is reached.

A decrease in demand

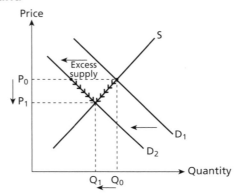

The market is initially at equilibrium at P_0Q_0. Demand decreases and shifts inwards. At the existing price, there is now excess supply. The price decreases, which increases the quantity demanded and decreases the quantity supplied until a new equilibrium price and quantity is reached.

An increase in supply

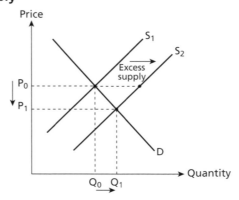

The market is initially at equilibrium at P_0Q_0. Supply increases and shifts outwards. At the existing price there is now excess supply. The price decreases, increasing the quantity demanded and decreasing the quantity supplied until a new equilibrium price and quantity is reached.

A decrease in supply

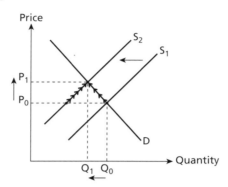

The market is initially at equilibrium at P_0Q_0. Supply decreases and shifts inwards. At the existing price, there is now excess demand. The price increases and this decreases the quantity demanded and increases the quantity supplied until a new equilibrium price and quantity is reached.

Summary

	Effect on equilibrium price	Effect on equilibrium quantity
outward shift (increase) in demand	increase	increase
inward shift (fall) in demand	decrease	decrease
outward shift (increase) in supply	decrease	increase
inward shift (fall) in supply	increase	decrease

The effect of an increase in indirect tax

An **indirect tax** increases producer costs and shifts supply inwards.

Specific unit tax

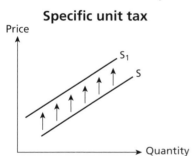

***Ad valorem* tax, e.g. of 10%**

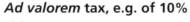
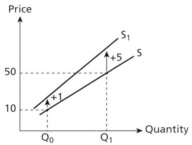

A specific tax adds a fixed amount to costs, so the supply curve moves in parallel.

An *ad valorem* tax adds a percentage to the costs. The higher the initial price, the greater the tax in $, e.g. 10% of $10 = $1, 10% of $50 = $5.

The effect of a production subsidy

A production **subsidy** reduces producer costs and shifts supply outwards.

Production subsidy

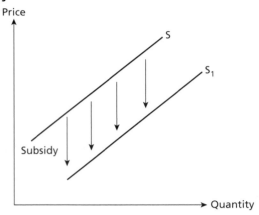

Quick test

A market is initially at equilibrium with supply curve S_0 and demand curve D_0.

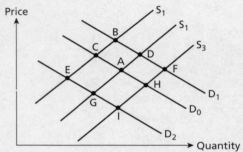

Select the change in market conditions that would explain the movement from:

1. A to B
2. A to C
3. A to D
4. A to E

   a) an outward shift in demand and inward shift in supply

   b) an outward shift in demand and outward shift in supply

   c) an inward shift in demand and inward shift in supply

   d) an inward shift in demand and outward shift in supply

   e) an inward shift in supply only

   f) an outward shift in supply only

   g) an inward shift in demand only

   h) an outward shift in demand only

Price elasticity of demand (PED)

Price elasticity of demand (PED) measures the percentage change in quantity demanded in relation to percentage change in price, all other factors unchanged.

$$PED = \frac{\% \text{ change in quantity demanded}}{\% \text{ change in price}}$$

The sign of the result shows the direction of movement. A negative result shows that the price and quantity demanded move in different directions, e.g. an increase in price reduces the quantity demanded or vice versa.

The size of the result shows how responsive the quantity demanded is to changes in price, e.g.

- if the PED value is 2, a 1% change in price leads to a 2 × 1% change in quantity demanded
- if the PED value is 0.2, a 1% change in price leads to a 0.2 × 1% change in quantity demanded.

Value (ignoring the sign)	Description	Explanation
infinity	completely price elastic	a given % change in price leads to an infinite change in quantity demanded
> 1	price elastic	a given % change in price leads to a greater % change in quantity demanded
= 1	unit elastic	a given % change in price leads to the same % change in quantity demanded
< 1	price inelastic	a given % change in price leads to a smaller % change in quantity demanded
0	completely price inelastic	a given % change in price leads to no change in quantity demanded

You must be able to:
- explain what is meant by the 'price elasticity' of demand
- interpret the significance of the value of the price elasticity of demand
- calculate the price elasticity of demand
- describe factors that influence the price elasticity of demand
- explain the difference between price elastic and price inelastic demand
- explain the significance of price elasticity of demand when making pricing decisions.

Revision tip

Remember that price elasticity shows how much the quantity demanded changes (as a %) compared to the change in price (as a %). Is the change in quantity demanded greater or smaller than the change in price?

Examples of price elasticity

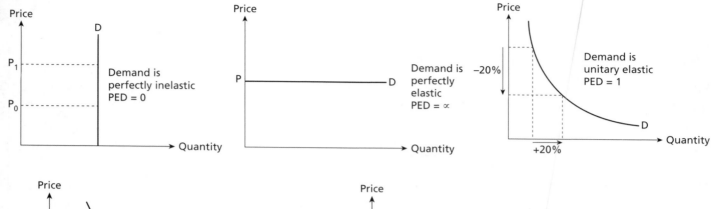

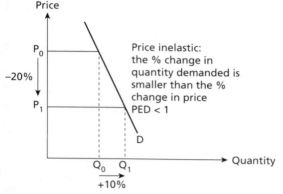

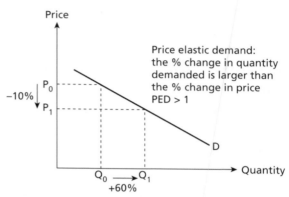

PED and revenue

Value	Price change	Effect on revenue	Explanation
price inelastic (< 1)	price increase	increases revenue (and spending)	• higher price per unit • % fall in quantity demanded is smaller than % increase in price
price inelastic (< 1)	price decrease	decreases revenue (and spending)	• lower price per unit • % rise in quantity demanded is smaller than % increase in price
price elastic (> 1)	price increase	decreases revenue (and spending)	• higher price per unit • % fall in quantity demanded is greater than % increase in price
price elastic (> 1)	price decrease	increases revenue (and spending)	• lower price per unit • % rise in quantity demanded is greater than % increase in price
unitary price elastic (= 1)	price increase or decrease	no change	% change in quantity demanded is the same as % change in price

When deciding whether to put the price up or down, a producer will consider the price elasticity of demand:

- if demand is price inelastic, the producer will increase the price to increase revenue
- if demand is price elastic, the producer will lower the price to increase revenue.

> **Revision tip**
>
> Remember, if you know the PED, you can estimate the effect of a price change on revenue. However, to understand the impact on profits, you would need to know what is happening to costs as well.

Example

A product has a price elasticity of demand of –2. The unit price is $40 and the quantity demanded is 20 units.

If the price increases by 10%, what is the effect on total revenue?

% price increase = $\left(\frac{10}{100}\right)$ × 40 = $4.

New price = $40 + $4 = $44

Quantity demanded will change by –2 × 10% = –20%

20% of 20 units = $\left(\frac{20}{100}\right)$ × 20 = 4

Quantity demanded = 20 – 4 = 16.

Revenue = price × quantity

Original revenue = $40 × 20 = $800

New revenue = $44 × 16 = $704

The 10% increase in price has led to a $96 fall in revenue because demand is price elastic.

You can use a formula triangle to help with these calculations:

$b = \frac{a}{c}$

$a = b \times c$

$c = \frac{a}{b}$

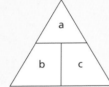

If a 10% increase in price leads to a 20% fall in quantity demanded, the PED is –2.

If you know two of the elements of the triangle, the third can be calculated:

PED = $\frac{-20}{+10}$ = –2

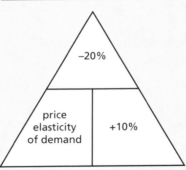

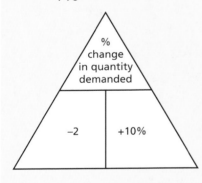

% change in quantity demanded = –2 × (+10) = –20%

Determinants of PED

Factor	More price inelastic if...
number of substitutes available	few are available (as consumers cannot easily switch)
branding	heavily branded (as consumers will not be sensitive to price)
percentage of income spent on the product	a small percentage is spent on the product (as consumers will not be sensitive to a price change if it does not have significant impact)
time	short term (as consumers will not immediately find substitutes to switch to)

Significance of PED

Understanding the PED enables **firms** to anticipate the impact of changes in price on the quantity demanded. This is important as it allows them to:

- plan stock and staff levels
- forecast sales, cash flow and profit.

A **government** will be interested in PED as it will affect the extent to which indirect taxes and subsidies have an impact on price and quantity. For example, if the government taxes cigarettes, by how much will the quantity demanded fall? This will have an impact on consumption and its tax revenue.

Quick test

1. State the equation for the price elasticity of demand.
2. What does it mean if demand is 'price inelastic'?
3. If the price elasticity of demand is −2.5 and price increases, will total revenue rise or fall?
4. Give **one** factor that can influence the price elasticity of demand of a product.
5. A product has a price elasticity of demand of −0.5. Sales are 200 units.
   If the price increases by 10%, what will the new level of sales be?

Price elasticity of supply (PES)

Price elasticity of supply (PES) measures the percentage change in quantity supplied in response to a percentage change in price.

$$PES = \frac{\% \text{ change in quantity supplied}}{\% \text{ change in price}}$$

The sign of the result shows the direction of movement. A positive result shows that the price and quantity supplied move in the same direction, e.g. an increase in price increases the quantity supplied or vice versa.

The size of the result shows how responsive the quantity supplied is to changes in price, e.g.

- if the PES value is 2, a 1% change in price leads to a 2 × 1% change in quantity supplied
- if the PES value is 0.2, a 1% change in price leads to a 0.2 × 1% change in quantity supplied.

> **You must be able to:**
> - explain what is meant by the 'price elasticity' of supply
> - understand the difference between price elastic and price inelastic supply
> - interpret the value of the price elasticity of supply
> - calculate the price elasticity of supply
> - explain the factors that influence the price elasticity of supply.

Value	Description	Explanation
infinity	completely price elastic	a given % change in price leads to an infinite change in quantity supplied
> 1	price elastic	a given % change in price leads to a greater % change in quantity supplied
= 1	unit elastic	a given % change in price leads to the same % change in quantity supplied
< 1	price inelastic	a given % change in price leads to a smaller % change in quantity supplied
0	completely price inelastic	a given % change in price has no effect on the quantity supplied

Examples of price elasticity

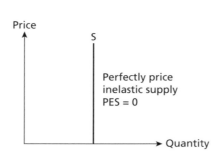

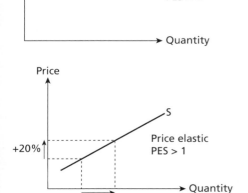

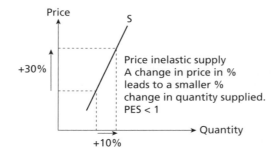

Example 1

The price of a product increases from $10 to $11. The quantity supplied increases from 5 units to 6 units. Is supply price elastic or price inelastic?

$$\% \text{ change} = \left(\frac{(\text{new value} - \text{old value})}{\text{old value}}\right) \times 100$$

$$\% \text{ change in quantity supplied} = \left(\frac{(6-5)}{5}\right) \times 100 = +20\%$$

$$\% \text{ change in price} = \left(\frac{(11-10)}{10}\right) \times 100 = +10\%$$

$$PES = \frac{+20}{+10} = +2$$

Supply is price elastic as the percentage change in quantity supplied is greater than the percentage change in price.

Example 2

The price of a product increases from $10 to $15. The quantity supplied increases from 5 units to 6 units. Is supply price elastic or price inelastic?

$$\% \text{ change in quantity supplied} = \left(\frac{(6-5)}{5}\right) \times 100 = +20\%$$

$$\text{Percentage change in price} = \left(\frac{(15-10)}{10}\right) \times 100 = +50\%$$

$$PES = \frac{+20}{+50} = +0.4$$

Supply is price inelastic as the change in quantity supplied is less than the percentage change in price.

Remember, you can use a formula triangle to help with these calculations.

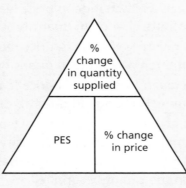

If a 10% increase in price leads to a 20% increase in quantity supplied, the PES is +2.

If you know two of the elements of the triangle, the third can be calculated.

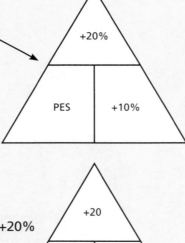

$$PES = \frac{+20}{+10} = +2$$

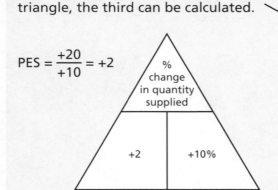

$$\% \text{ change in quantity supplied} = 2 \times (+10) = +20\%$$

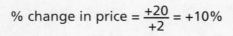

$$\% \text{ change in price} = \frac{+20}{+2} = +10\%$$

Determinants of PES

Factors	More price elastic if...
capacity	there is capacity available (as can easily produce more)
factor substitution	it is easy to switch factors from one production to another
time	long term (as it is possible to switch more factors of production from other industries into producing in this industry)
stocks	a business has high levels of stock (as it can more easily supply more given a price change)

Quick test

1. State the equation for the price elasticity of supply.

2. What does it mean if supply is price inelastic?

3. The price elasticity of supply of a product is +2.5. If the price increases by 5%, what will be the percentage increase in quantity supplied?

4. Give **one** factor that can influence the price elasticity of supply of a product.

5. The price elasticity of supply of a product is +0.5. There are 200 units supplied. If the price increases by 2%, how many units will now be supplied?

Market economic system

Market economic system

The **private sector** refers to businesses owned by private individuals. These are assumed to profit maximise. The **public sector** refers to businesses owned by the government. These may have social objectives.

In a **free market economy**, the basic economic questions (what to produce, who to produce it for and how to produce it) are solved by the decisions of firms and households in the private sector.

In a **command (or planned) economy**, the basic economic questions are solved by the government allocating resources.

In a **mixed economy** there is both a private sector and public sector. The basic economic questions are solved partly by the free market and partly by the government.

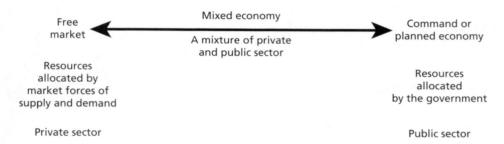

If a government takes over a private sector business, it is called **nationalisation**. If a business is sold, so it is no longer under government control and is privately owned, it is called **privatisation**.

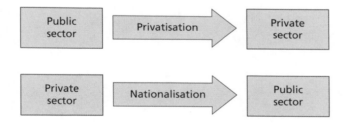

> **You must be able to:**
> - explain the difference between the private and public sectors
> - understand the advantages and disadvantages of the free market economy
> - understand the advantages and disadvantages of the planned (command) economy.

> **Revision tip**
>
> All economies are mixed to some degree. The extent to which the government intervenes is where they differ.
>
> What is provided by the public sector in one country may be provided by the private sector in another. For example, in the UK, healthcare is mainly provided by the government and is generally free of charge. In the USA, more healthcare is provided by the free market and is paid for.

Advantages and disadvantages of the market economic system

Command (planned) economy

Advantages	Disadvantages
can pursue social objectives and take account of **social costs** and benefits	removes profit incentive, which may lead to a lack of innovation and enterprise
can overcome market failures, such as **monopoly power** and the lack of provision of **public goods**	government has to make many decisions and may be dealing with too much information to make the right ones

Free market economy

Advantages	Disadvantages
incentive to be profitable means firms innovate, which leads to new products and new ways of doing things	may only focus on private costs and benefits and not take into account social costs and benefits
decisions are made by individual firms and households – does not need a government to decide what to do, so reduces costs	price can fluctuate as supply and demand conditions change – this can cause instability and make planning difficult

Quick test

1. What is meant by 'the private sector'?
2. What is meant by 'the public sector'?
3. Explain how the objectives of a public sector organisation may differ from the private sector.
4. What is meant by a 'mixed economy'?
5. Give **one** advantage of a free market economy compared to a planned economy.

Market failure

Causes and consequences of market failure

Market failures are failings that occur within the free market.

Public goods

Public goods, such as defence, are:

* **non-diminishable** – if someone consumes more of a product, it does not reduce the amount available for others
* **non-excludable** – you cannot prevent someone from consuming the product.

This creates the **free rider problem**, where people use a public good or resource without paying their share of the cost.

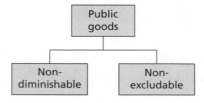

Merit goods

Merit goods are better for the individual than the individual may appreciate. For example, young people may not value education enough, so the government may need to make it compulsory to ensure they have it.

Demerit goods

Demerit goods are worse for the individual that the individual may appreciate, e.g. cigarettes and drugs. The government may intervene to stop individuals doing things that are bad for them.

Private benefits and private costs versus social benefits and social costs

In the private sector, businesses will only take account of the benefits they get (e.g. the revenue from sales) or the costs that they generate (e.g. the amount they have to pay for labour and land).

These private benefits and costs may not reflect the full costs and benefits to society, i.e. the decisions taken by private firms may not be the best decisions for society as a whole.

For example, the production process of a business may generate external costs, such as noise and pollution. A private firm would not take account of these and, therefore, would over produce. The government may need to intervene to make businesses aware of these costs, e.g. by taxing them.

The social costs = private costs + external costs

Similarly, if a business sells a cure for a disease, it will only measure the private benefits, i.e. the revenue it earns. However, if the workforce is healthier and fitter, it will be more productive and this will benefit society as a whole. There is an external benefit of producing these cures.

The social benefit = private benefit + external benefit

You must be able to:
* define 'market failure'
* explain different types of market failure, such as public goods and merit goods
* understand external costs and benefits.

Revision tip

There can be differences between private costs and benefits and social costs and benefits in both production and consumption.

Revision tip

Some aspects of monopolies may be undesirable for society. However, some aspects may be positive. This is why governments usually make sure they have the right to investigate monopolies, but do not always assume they are bad.

social benefit	private benefit + external benefit
social cost	private cost + external cost

External cost / benefit	Example
external cost of production	pollution; traffic congestion
external cost of consumption	the effect of smoking on others (passive smoking)
external benefit of production	if more people cycle to work, it reduces congestion on the roads and reduces the journey time for those who still drive
external benefit of consumption	by getting an inoculation you protect yourself and others; by getting training you improve your own productivity and earnings, but also the output of the economy (providing more goods for others)

Monopoly power

Monopoly power occurs when one firm dominates a market, e.g. if its sales are more than 25% of all of the sales in an industry. In a pure monopoly, there is only one firm in the industry.

A monopoly can be a price maker, i.e. it can push up the price. In a monopoly, the price is likely to be higher than in a competitive market and the quantity less – consumers pay more and less is produced overall.

Quick test

1. What is meant by a 'market failure'?
2. What is meant by a 'merit good'?
3. Explain why monopoly power is a market failure.
4. Explain why private and social costs may differ.
5. State the **two** features of a public good.

Mixed economic system

Government intervention to address market failure

A government may intervene in an economy to overcome market failures:

Minimum and maximum prices

A **maximum price** is set by the government to limit the price that can be charged in a market. For example, the government may set a maximum rent for properties to try and keep rents lower than they may otherwise be in a free market.

A maximum price set below the equilibrium price will create a shortage, i.e. a greater quantity demanded than supplied.

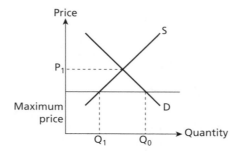

A **minimum price** is set by the government to limit how low the price can go in a market. For example, the government may set a minimum wage to try and keep wages higher than they may otherwise be in a free market.

A minimum price set above the equilibrium price will create a surplus, i.e. a greater quantity supplied than demanded.

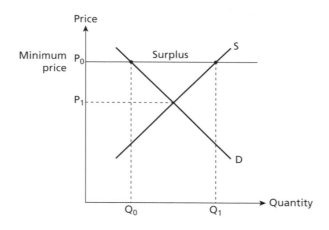

These price controls can be used in different markets, e.g. setting a minimum wage in the labour market, a maximum value of currency in the currency market or a minimum price for a product.

Indirect taxation

Indirect taxes may be imposed on producers to make them take account of the external costs of their production (e.g. producer taxes) or to make consumers aware of the external costs of what they are

You must be able to:
- explain the ways in which a government may intervene in the market
- explain the effects of minimum and maximum prices
- explain the effects of indirect taxes and subsidies
- understand the meaning of nationalisation.

> **Revision tip**
>
> If the maximum price is above the equilibrium price, it has no effect on the equilibrium price and quantity.

> **Revision tip**
>
> If the minimum price is below the equilibrium price, it has no effect on the equilibrium price and quantity.

consuming (e.g. a tax on cigarettes). By increasing costs, the aim is to reduce the equilibrium output to the optimum level for society.

Subsidies

Subsidies may be used to pay producers to reduce their costs if there are social benefits to production (e.g. to encourage energy-saving measures to help society as a whole) or they may be paid to consumers to encourage consumption where there is an external benefit to consuming.

Regulation

The government may introduce rules and **regulations** to make businesses behave in certain ways, e.g. to ensure that businesses label products and take account of health and safety measures and to ensure that monopolies do not abuse their power and push up prices.

Buffer stocks

Sometimes government may want to keep the price of a product stable. In this case, if supply is high and the price is likely to fall, the government intervenes and buys up the excess supply. This is called **buffer stock**. If in the future supply falls and there is a shortage, the government can sell the buffer stock to increase supply and keep the price stable. Buffer stock systems are often used in agricultural markets where the supply can shift a lot due to weather or disease and the government wants to keep food prices stable for producers and consumers.

Nationalisation

The government could take control of an industry to ensure it pursues social objectives. This is called **nationalisation**. Alternatively, if the government thinks a business would be more efficient with a profit incentive, it may privatise it. **Privatisation** occurs when a business is transferred from the public sector to the private sector.

Short run and long run

One reason for government intervention is that it wants to plan long term. Many consumers and firms will focus on short-term costs and benefits rather than long-term cost and benefits. For example, firms will consider the immediate cost of buying energy but, in a free market, will not take account of the long-term impact on the environment (from using up stocks of non-renewable resources and the environmental damage caused), whereas the government may consider the benefits of conserving resources for future generations.

Quick test

1. Explain how a minimum price set higher than the equilibrium price affects the price and quantity in a market.
2. Explain how a maximum price set lower than the equilibrium price affects the price and quantity in a market.
3. Explain how nationalisation may reduce market failures.
4. Explain how indirect taxation may be used to reduce a market failure.
5. Explain how an indirect tax may affect the equilibrium price and quantity in a market.

Exam-style practice questions

1   Which is **most** likely to make demand for a product more price inelastic?   [1]

   a)   a higher proportion of income spent on the product

   b)   an increase in the number of close substitutes

   c)   more awareness of the availability of alternative options

   d)   stronger branding

2   What does it mean if the price elasticity of demand is –0.2?   [1]

   a)   demand is price elastic and total revenue decreases as price increases

   b)   demand is price elastic and total revenue increases as price increases

   c)   demand is price inelastic and total revenue decreases as price increases

   d)   demand is price inelastic and total revenue increases as price increases

3   What is **most** likely to encourage domestic producers to grow more wheat?   [1]

   a)   increasing the sales tax on wheat

   b)   more subsidies to wheat producers

   c)   removing guaranteed minimum prices for wheat

   d)   removing quotas on imported wheat

4   Which is an example of an external cost?   [1]

   a)   a company's labour costs

   b)   the cost of industrial pollution

   c)   the cost of supplies

   d)   the cost of a takeover

5   What is **most** likely to lead to an increase in the equilibrium price and a decrease in the equilibrium quantity?   [1]

   a)   a decrease in demand

   b)   a decrease in supply

   c)   an increase in demand

   d)   an increase in supply

6 What is **most** likely to explain a movement from B to A? [1]

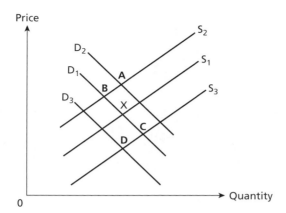

a) a decrease in indirect taxes

b) a decrease in spending on marketing

c) an increase in input costs

d) an increase in the price of a substitute product

7 What is **most** likely to explain a movement from B to C? [1]

a) a decrease in indirect taxes

b) a decrease in spending on marketing

c) an increase in input costs

d) an increase in the price of a substitute product

8 **The property market**

In 2017, the Organisation for Economic Cooperation and Development (OECD) warned that property prices were very high in a number of countries and could collapse in the future. In several economies property prices had increased significantly in preceding years and there was a danger that they might fall quite suddenly by 10% or more.

In Canada, for example, average property prices had doubled since the start of the century. Prices in London were also particularly high. Of 30 economists surveyed, 20 predicted that house prices in London would stay stable or fall in the near future.

For most people buying a house is the biggest expenditure of their lives. They have to borrow to afford it and then repay over many years. The Royal Institution of Surveyors in the UK reported that the number of new buyer inquiries was very low. There were concerns over the state of the UK economy and it seemed to be affecting people's willingness to spend large sums on housing. Also, employees in the UK were generally experiencing very slow wage growth – with wages increasing at a slower rate than prices, there had been a fall in consumer purchasing power.

Banks were keen to reduce the risks of lending. Changes were made by banks in many countries, which required house buyers to provide bigger deposits and restricted the amount they could borrow. The number of new properties on the market was also at a record low.

Fig. 1: Annual percentage change in house prices and the growth of incomes in leading economies (1970–2015)

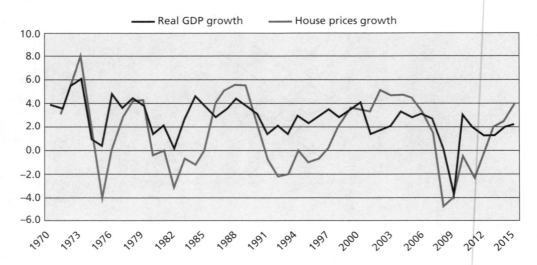

Fig. 2: Annual percentage change in UK house prices

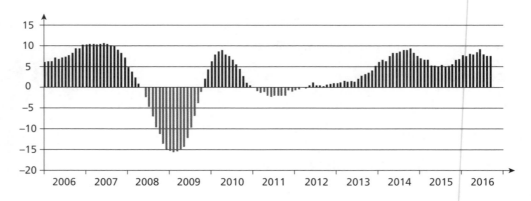

a) Explain the effect on the purchasing power of a consumer if wages are constant but prices rise. [2]

b) What risks do banks take when lending to house buyers? [2]

c) Explain why the apparent relationship between house prices and national income growth in Fig. 1. might exist. [4]

d) With reference to Fig. 2, explain what was happening to UK house prices in 2008 and 2009. [2]

e) Explain the factors that may influence the demand for property apart from income. [4]

f) Using a supply and demand diagram, explain why house prices might have been so high in the UK in 2017. [4]

g) Discuss the possible effects on an economy of a fall in property prices. [6]

h) Discuss whether buying a house is a good investment for households. [6]

9 In 2017, Europe experienced a shortage of butter which has affected its price. This shortage was caused by falling milk production in many countries and a lack of stocks to use up. The supply of butter cannot increase easily because many dairy farms in Europe and Brazil are suffering from a shortage of young cows to bring into the herd to produce the milk needed. This was partly because in recent years, production had been too high and many governments in Europe had introduced voluntary output cuts and compensated farmers for not producing milk.

a) Define 'shortage'. [2]

b) Explain two factors that may influence the supply of products. [4]

c) Analyse the effect of a decrease in supply on the equilibrium price and output. Show the effect using a supply and demand diagram. [6]

d) Discuss whether a government should introduce a maximum price for products. [8]

10 In 2017 in Scotland, the government discussed a minimum price for tobacco. This policy was intended to reduce overconsumption of tobacco. Critics said that the effect on consumption would be limited because of the price elasticity of demand.

a) Define a 'minimum price'. [2]

b) Explain the factors that might influence the price elasticity of demand of tobacco. [4]

c) Using a demand and supply diagram, analyse the likely effect of introducing a minimum price in a market. [6]

d) Discuss the extent to which knowledge of price elasticity of demand is of use to a government. [8]

11 Although Singapore is a relatively free market economy, the government does intervene to influence the allocation of resources. The government of Singapore has recently introduced tougher standards to limit vehicle emissions to achieve cleaner and greener vehicles in the country. Air pollution is a big environmental health risk, particularly for heart diseases and strokes. Vehicles are also taxed in Singapore to reduce their usage.

a) Describe how resources are allocated in a free market economy. [2]

b) Explain using a diagram how pollution can lead to inefficiency in a market economy. [4]

c) Analyse how taxes can be used to reduce the inefficiency caused by pollution in a free market. [6]

d) Discuss whether introducing tougher standards on vehicle emissions is a better way of reducing pollution in an economy than taxation. [8]

Money and banking

Money

Money has many forms, including notes, coins and bank accounts. It is:

- a store of value – it can be saved and will retain value
- a unit of account – it is used to measure the value of goods and services
- a medium of exchange – individuals and firms are willing to trade goods and services for it because they know they can use it later to purchase other items
- a standard of deferred payment – many transactions in an economy are on credit; individuals and firms are willing to sell items on credit and be paid later because money is a store of value.

Banking

Commercial banks

Commercial banks are the high street banks, such as Barclays and HSBC. The main functions of commercial banks are to:

- accept deposits from savers
- lend to households and firms
- provide efficient means of payment.

Commercial banks are **financial intermediaries** and play a key role in moving funds from those who have surplus funds (lenders / savers) to those who want those funds (borrowers).

Central banks

A **central bank** manages a country's currency, money supply and **interest rates** on behalf of the government. It is responsible for monetary policy.

The main responsibilities of a central bank are:

- issuing banknotes and managing the currency
- providing monetary stability, e.g. a central bank may be tasked with delivering stable prices, which it will aim to achieve by setting interest rates
- providing financial stability and ensuring that financial institutions can be trusted, e.g. if necessary the bank intervenes to manage failing financial organisations
- banker to the government, i.e. it helps the government to raise money
- a lender of the last resort to the banking system.

> You must be able to:
> - understand the forms and functions of money
> - explain the role of central banks
> - understand the role of commercial banks
> - understand the role of stock exchanges.

Quick test

1. Explain why money is 'a store of value'.
2. State **two** functions of money other than being a store of value.
3. Give **two** functions of a commercial bank.
4. Explain the role of a central bank.

Households

Income

Households earn income from work. What they spend out of their income on goods and services is called **consumption**. What they do not spend out of their income is called **savings**. To increase their funds, households may borrow money.

You must be able to:
- explain the different motives for spending, saving and borrowing
- explain the factors that can influence spending and saving.

Income by age

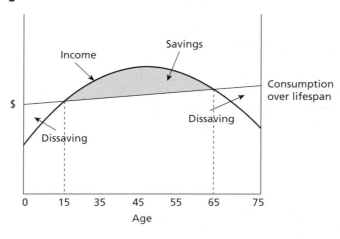

Spending

Households spend some or all of their income. In some cases, they borrow so they can spend more than their income. Households may spend on essentials, such as food and housing, or non-essentials, such as eating out or holidays.

Consumer spending (or expenditure) patterns will change according to different factors:

The stage in an individual's life cycle

When an individual leaves school or university, they may start spending on rent for accommodation. If they start a family, they may have to spend on specific items, such as school clothes. This is very different from what a retired individual spends their income on.

The time of year

There may be seasonal patterns to spending. For example, an individual may spend more in summer when on holiday.

Income

If an individual has a low income, most of their spending is likely to be on essentials, such as rent and food. As income increases, individuals may start to spend more on eating out and holidays.

Savings

Households save to finance future spending, e.g. they save now to finance a holiday or a deposit on a car or house later. The amount that households save depends on different factors:

Interest rates

The rate of interest is the return that individuals receive by putting money in a bank. For example, if the interest rate is 2% a year, an individual who saves $100 in the bank will receive an interest payment of $2 at the end of the year. If the interest rate is 5%, the individual will receive $5.

If interest rates increase, there is a greater incentive for individuals to save their income. If interest rates decrease, there is less incentive to save as the rewards are lower, so individuals are more likely to spend their income.

Income

The higher an individual's income, the more they tend to save. When incomes are low, all or most of the money is spent on essential purchases. As incomes increase, households have more than they need for essential purchases and can start to save.

Their stage in an individual's life cycle

Generally, younger people save less. This may be because they have less income, but it may also be because they plan less for the future. In middle age, people earn more and are able save more. They are also saving for retirement. Retirement households may **dissave**, i.e. spend more than they earn, as they use the savings from earlier in their lives.

Confidence in the future

If households are worried about whether they will have a job in the future, they may save more for security.

Government incentives

Governments may offer incentives to encourage more saving, e.g. a tax incentive to those who save for their retirement.

Borrowing

People borrow when they want to buy something but do not have enough money to pay for it. They borrow and pay back over time. People may borrow because:

- the sum required is large, e.g. people may borrow to buy a house (this is called a **mortgage**) and then repay over a long period of time (often 25 years)
- of timing, e.g. there may be times during the year (such as celebrations or summer holidays) when there are major outflows and, to finance this or to provide finances after this, it may be necessary to borrow money short term.

Overdrafts versus loans

An **overdraft** occurs when a household can borrow up to a certain amount agreed with a bank. Interest is paid on how much is actually borrowed. A **loan** occurs when a fixed amount is borrowed and repaid at agreed rates.

If a household knows exactly how much it wants to borrow (e.g. to buy a car), it may take out a loan and agree in advance how much it will repay in instalments (e.g. over five years).

If a household may need money (e.g. in case of high levels of spending whilst on holiday), it may organise an overdraft. Interest is only paid on what is used. However, interest is high so, if households know how much they need, a loan is better.

Fixed-rate and variable-rate borrowing

A **fixed-rate loan** is where interest repayments are agreed at the start. A **variable-rate loan** is where the interest repayments may vary as interest rates in the economy change.

The amount households can borrow depends on:

*   whether they can find others to lend to them (this may depend on what security or collateral they can provide to potential lenders)
*   the interest rate, i.e. the cost of borrowing money and the reward for saving money – the higher the interest rate, the higher the cost of borrowing and the higher the reward for saving (this usually leads to less spending and more savings)
*   consumer confidence – if consumers think that the economy is doing well and that they are likely to keep their job and may even get a pay increase, then they are more likely to spend; if they think they may lose their job, they are more likely to save
*   what they wish to buy and how important they think it is to have it now and repay over time.

Quick test

1. What is meant by an 'interest rate'?
2. State **two** factors, other than interest rates, that may affect the spending of a household.
3. Give **two** motives for saving.
4. Give **one** reason why expenditure patterns vary between households.
5. What is the difference between an overdraft and a loan?

Workers

Choice of occupation

An individual's choice of job will depend on factors such as:

- the wage rate – usually when the wage rate increases more people are willing to work in an industry
- non-monetary factors, e.g. is the job very repetitive or dangerous and what are working conditions like?
- skills – to be a doctor, for example, requires very good qualifications and high levels of training, which limits the number of people who can do the job
- the alternatives and the opportunity cost.

Wage determination

When an individual first starts earning, their income is likely to be relatively low. Individuals are often dissaving. Over time, individuals will hopefully earn more as they:

- gain more skills and can do more skilled work
- get promoted to higher-earning positions.

Typically, individuals begin to save as they earn more. When individuals retire, they often use up their savings to enable them to consume more than their income at that time.

Reasons for differences in earnings

The earnings of an individual will depend on supply and demand conditions. Earnings are likely to be high if:

- supply is limited, e.g. if it takes many years to train to do the job (such as architect or lawyer)
- demand is high, e.g. the business will earn large sums from selling their output (such as top footballers).

Typically, skilled workers will earn more than unskilled workers because the supply is more limited and the workers' output is worth more, so demand is higher.

Earnings in the public sector tend to be lower than in the private sector. This is because governments usually have limited funds. Much of the output (e.g. health and education) is not sold or is sold at a lower price because maximising profits is not an objective. As a result, output does not generate the revenue to pay high wages. However, lower pay is sometimes compensated for by greater job security and good pensions when people retire.

Private sector output is sold in markets and earns money for the business. If demand for the product is higher, the business can pay its employees more.

Women often earn less than men. In some cases this is due to discrimination – employers do not always treat women in the same way as men, even though most countries have legislation requiring them to do so.

> You must be able to:
> - understand the factors that influence an individual's choice of occupation
> - understand the factors that influence earnings
> - understand what is meant by specialisation.

Earnings in manufacturing will typically be higher than in agriculture. This is because it is easier to increase productivity in manufacturing through investment in technology and capital. This enables workers to produce more and, assuming there is a market for the products, it enables them to generate more money for the business. As a result, the business can reward them more highly.

Trade unions are organisations that represent employees and bargain with employers. By representing groups of employees, trade unions have more power than an individual would alone. This can enable a trade union to increase the wages of its members.

Specialisation

Specialisation occurs when jobs are divided into smaller tasks and employees are trained to do one of these specific tasks.

For the worker, specialisation means:

- it is relatively easy to learn what to do
- by repeating the same task, they can become very productive, which may lead to more earnings.

However, the work is repetitive and not very challenging.

For the business, specialisation means:

- it is relatively easy to recruit and train workers to do the jobs
- productivity may be high through repetition.

However, workers may be demotivated as the work can become boring and they may leave to get more interesting jobs.

Quick test

1. State **two** factors that influence an individual's choice of occupation.
2. What is the likely effect of a limited supply of labour on the wages paid in an industry?
3. What is the likely effect of a high demand for labour on the wages paid in an industry?
4. Explain why the wages paid in the public sector are often lower than in the private sector.
5. Explain why skilled workers usually earn more than unskilled workers.

Trade unions

Trade unions and their role in the economy

Trade unions are organisations formed to represent employees' interests and act as a counterbalance to the power of employers.

Trade unions may be involved in decision-making. Managers may:

- inform trade unions of decisions (i.e. tell them)
- consult with trade unions (i.e. ask for their opinion)
- negotiate with trade unions (i.e. bargain with them).

Trade unions may be involved in a range of issues, such as:

- redundancies – these occur when workers lose their jobs because the jobs no longer exist
- dismissals – these occur when a worker loses their job because they are no longer competent at undertaking it
- training
- working conditions
- payment
- terms and conditions of employment
- changes to job descriptions.

The actions that trade unions take include:

- representing employees' views in meetings
- representing employees' views to the media
- undertaking a **work to rule**, i.e. when employees do exactly what is in their contract and no more – over time people are often expected to do more than is in the job description, so if unions force a work to rule, it often slows up the rate of work as people revert to what they were originally expected to do
- an overtime ban, i.e. when employees work the number of hours in their contract but do not volunteer for overtime – in many businesses, overtime work is a common way of making sure they can cope with sudden increases in orders, so a reduction in overtime will increase the time taken for work to be done
- a **strike**, i.e. when employees withdraw their labour – there is no production (on strike employees do not receive pay from their employers)
- restricting supply – in some countries, trade unions insist that employees belong to a trade union, which can restrict supply.

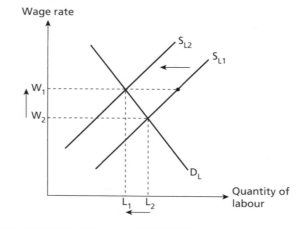

You must be able to:
- explain the role of trade unions
- understand the actions that trade unions can take
- understand the advantages and disadvantages of trade union membership.

The advantages and disadvantages of trade union membership

The benefits of joining a trade union for employees are that it:

- provides greater protection (employees have greater power if they act as a group)
- provides expertise, e.g. legal advice
- will bargain for better pay and conditions.

The disadvantages of trade union membership are that:

- there is a cost to join
- employees may prefer to bargain individually
- the trade union may take actions that an individual employee disagrees with.

Trade unions can help managers:

- find solutions to problems
- gain the agreement and cooperation of employees
- understand issues from employees' perspectives.

Trade unions may cause problems for managers by:

- pushing up wages and costs
- opposing changes, e.g. to increase productivity
- taking strike action, so output and revenue is lost.

Quick test

1. What is a trade union?
2. What is it called when employees withdraw their labour?
3. What term is used to describe the action taken by employees who will only do what is in their contracts?
4. What is it called when employees lose their jobs because there is no longer a demand for them?
5. State **one** benefit of trade unions to a business.

Firms

Sectors of the economy

Firms may be operating in the:

- **primary sector** – these firms are involved in farming and the extractive industries, such as oil and coal
- **secondary sector** – these firms take raw materials and process them, e.g. manufacturing
- **tertiary (service) sector** – these firms provide services, e.g. education and banking.

Small firms

The size of a firm can be measured by:

- its sales (turnover)
- what it owns (assets)
- the number of employees.

Other measures may also be appropriate depending on the nature of the business, e.g. the number of outlets (for a retail business) or the number of lorries (for a transportation business).

Small firms can make decisions fast, be innovative and create new products. However, they:

- lack market power
- may lack experience
- may lack the assets needed to raise funds
- may have high unit costs, as they lack economies of scale.

Causes of growth of firms

Firms may grow:

- internally, by selling more goods and services and investing the profits made
- externally, by joining (integrating) with another business – this could be through:
    - a **merger** – two or more firms join together to become one business
    - a **takeover** (or acquisition) – one business gains control of another.

Mergers

The types of integration are:

- **horizontal** – firms at the same stage of production join together, e.g. one car manufacturer joins with another car manufacturer
- **backward vertical** – a firm joins with another firm at an earlier stage of the same production process, e.g. a car manufacturer joins with a tyre manufacturer
- **forward vertical** – a firm joins with another business at a later stage (closer to the consumer) of the same production process, e.g. a car manufacturer joins with a car dealership

You must be able to:
- explain the different sectors of the economy
- understand how to measure the size of firms
- understand the advantages and disadvantages of being a small firm
- explain the different forms of business growth and their advantages and disadvantages
- describe how internal and external economies of scale can affect a business.

Revision tip

As economies develop, their resources tend to move from the primary sector into the secondary sector and then into the tertiary sector.

Revision tip

The motives for integration depend on the type of merger or takeover.

- **conglomerate integration** – a firm joins with a business in a different sector, e.g. a car rental company joins with a food hotel chain.

Type of integration	Motive
horizontal integration	• to remove competitors • to gain market share • to gain cost advantage by being bigger and getting better prices from suppliers
forward vertical integration	• to gain and secure access to the market, e.g. a business can sell through its own outlets
backward vertical integration	• to secure supplies – by owning a supplier, a firm can reduce costs and ensure quality
conglomerate integration	• to spread risk by operating in different markets, so less vulnerable to changes in sales in one market

Economies and diseconomies of scale

Internal economies of scale

Internal economies of scale occur when unit costs (or average costs) fall as a firm increases the scale of its production.

These may be due to

- purchasing economies – cost savings through bulk buying
- marketing economies – savings on advertising and marketing through having more power when negotiating
- technical economies – cost savings through use of mass production techniques
- risk-bearing economies – these occur when a business operates in different markets (geographically or product), because there is less risk of a fall in sales; if sales are affected in one market they may not be so affected in other markets, so sales are generally more stable and costs can be spread over more units than a business that is reliant on one market
- managerial economies – these occur for two reasons:
  - the number of managers will not grow at the same rate as output, e.g. output may double but it may be possible for the same manager to oversee the business, so the costs of the manager can be spread over more units
  - as the business grows, specialist managers can be employed in areas such as marketing and human resources, which can lead to better and more efficient decision-making.

Internal diseconomies of scale

Internal diseconomies of scale occur when unit costs rise as a firm increases the scale if its production, e.g. due to communication, coordination and control problems.

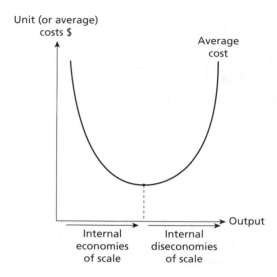

External economies of scale

External economies of scale occur when the unit costs are lower at every level of output. This is due to factors outside of the business itself. For example:

- if the whole industry grows, there may be a growth in specialist suppliers and training providers
- being located in an area where there is already a trained workforce reduces training costs, e.g. a computing business locating in Silicon Valley can benefit from all the skills and suppliers already in this area.

 Revision tip

Remember that internal economies of scale occur when the scale of production of the individual business increases. External economies are due to factors outside the business and reduce unit costs at all levels of output.

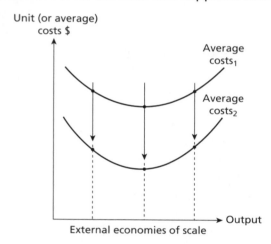

External economies of scale

Quick test

1. State one way in which the size of a business may be measured.
2. State **one** type of production in the primary sector and **one** type of production in the secondary sector.
3. Explain the difference between a merger and a takeover.
4. Explain the difference between backward vertical integration and forward vertical integration.
5. Define 'internal economies of scale'.
6. Explain **one** possible reason for horizontal integration.

Firms and production

Demand for factors of production

The factors of production are land, labour, capital and enterprise. The overall demand for factors of production depends on the demand for the final good or service, i.e. the demand for a factor of production is a **derived demand**. For example, labour is demanded because there is a need to produce – if there was no demand for the products, the business would not need labour.

The demand for any particular factor of production will depend on:

- what is being produced
- the availability and price of the factors of production.

For example, medical advice has traditionally relied on a doctor (labour), although improved technology means more diagnoses may now be carried out via computers and machines (capital). Greater demand for education typically requires more teachers (labour). By comparison, greater demand for chemicals or soft drinks requires investment in factories (land and capital).

If labour is readily available and cheap, a business may produce using a high amount of labour. If labour is expensive and takes a long time to recruit, a business may look for ways of producing with more capital.

Labour-intensive and capital-intensive production

Some forms of production are labour intensive, i.e. labour is the main factor of production. For example, hairdressing and accountancy are labour-intensive processes. Labour-intensive processes generally require a relatively high level of skills and are quite flexible to the different needs of customers.

Other processes are more capital intensive, i.e. capital is the main factor of production. For example, a bottling plant or car production process has high levels of investment in machinery and relatively little human input. These processes require heavy investment. Sometimes these processes are inflexible, i.e. they produce high quantities of standard products. However, developments in technology mean that the variety of products that can be produced is increasing.

> **You must be able to:**
> - explain what influences the demand for factors of production
> - understand the difference between labour-intensive and capital-intensive production
> - explain the difference between production and productivity.

Production and productivity

Production measures the total output of a business. **Productivity** measures output in relation to the inputs used to produce it. Both are measured in units.

$$\text{Productivity} = \frac{\text{output}}{\text{input}}$$

For example, if 200 units are produced by 40 employees:

$$\text{Labour productivity} = \frac{\text{output}}{\text{number of employees}} = \frac{200}{40} = 5 \text{ units per employee}$$

Businesses are very interested in productivity because it measures how well its resources are being used. An increase in productivity means:

- more units can be produced with the same inputs, which should increase sales and revenue
- the same output can be produced with fewer inputs, which should reduce costs.

The productivity of the workforce will depend on factors such as:

- the quantity and quality of capital equipment they have to work with
- the way their work is organised
- the training they have received
- their level of motivation.

Managers will try to increase productivity by:

- investing in equipment and technology
- using different rewards to motivate workers
- organising work in different ways to make it more efficient
- investing in training

Quick test

1. State the **four** factors of production.
2. State the equation for labour productivity.
3. The output of a business is 400 units. The number of employees is 80. What is the labour productivity?
4. State **two** factors that influence labour productivity.
5. Explain why productivity is important for managers.

Firms' costs, revenue and objectives

Costs of production

Costs are the charges that a business has to pay to produce. Types of cost include:

- **Total cost (TC)** = fixed costs + variable costs
- **Fixed costs (FC)**, e.g. rent and interest on a loan, do not change with the level of output; they can change (e.g. rent can be increased), but do not change with output
- **Variable costs (VC)**, e.g. the cost of materials used in production, do change with the level of output.

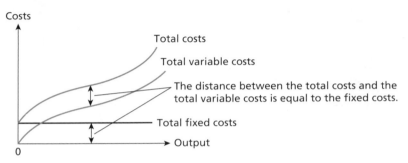

Variable costs increase with output. In the diagram above, they increase by less with each unit initially and then by more as the business keeps producing more (which is why the 'variable costs' line gets steeper). This is because adding more labour to fixed factors of production will eventually lead to less extra productivity in the short-run – there will be too many people and not enough equipment. This is known as the Law of Diminishing Returns. With less productivity from extra employees, the variable cost of a unit increases.

Total costs are found by adding the fixed costs to the variable costs.

Average cost (AC) is a measure of the cost per unit.

$$\text{Average cost} = \frac{\text{total cost}}{\text{output}}$$

Average cost = average fixed cost + average variable cost

AC = AFC + AVC

$$\frac{\text{total cost}}{\text{output}} = \frac{\text{fixed cost}}{\text{output}} + \frac{\text{variable cost}}{\text{output}}$$

Average fixed costs fall as output increases

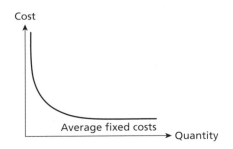

> **Revision tip**

Remember that fixed costs can change, e.g. rents can increase. It simply means that they do not change with output, e.g. if there are more people entering a shop and buying clothes, it does not affect the rent.

In the long run, all costs are variable as all resources can be changed.

Output (units)	Fixed costs ($)	Variable costs ($) if VC are $500 per unit	Total costs = fixed costs + variable costs ($)	Average cost = $\frac{\text{total cost}}{\text{output}}$ ($)
0	10 000	0	10 000	n/a
10	10 000	5000	15 000	1500
20	10 000	10 000	20 000	1000
30	10 000	15 000	25 000	833.33

 Revision tip

As output increases, the fixed costs are spread over more units and the average fixed cost falls. This means the average total cost is mainly made up of average variable cost.

Item	Meaning	Equation
total cost	fixed costs + variable costs	$TC = FC + VC$
average (unit) cost	average cost per unit = average fixed cost + average variable cost	$AC = \dfrac{TC}{Q} = AFC + AVC$
average fixed cost	fixed cost per unit	$AFC = \dfrac{FC}{Q}$
average variable cost	variable cost per unit	$AVC = \dfrac{VC}{Q}$

 Revision tip

Costs are what the business has to pay. Revenue is what is paid to the business for its products. Profit is the difference between revenue and costs.

Revenue

Revenue (or total revenue) measures the income of the business. It is equal to the spending (or expenditure) of consumers.

Total revenue = TR = price per unit × number of units sold = P × Q

Average revenue (AR) is the revenue per unit. It is equal to the price.
AR = P

Profit

Profit is the difference between revenue and costs.
Profit = revenue – costs (or TR – TC)

If the price is held constant and more is sold at the same price, the total revenue will be a straight line.

Price $	Output $	Total revenue $
10	0	0
10	1	10
10	2	20
10	3	30
10	4	40
10	5	50
10	6	60
10	7	70

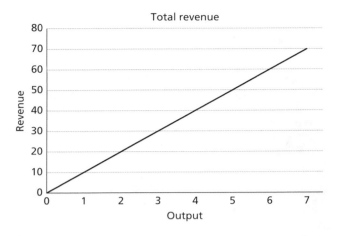

Total revenue

If the demand curve is downward sloping, then to sell more the price must fall. This means the total revenue curve will not be a straight line. It will actually increase at a decreasing rate because to sell more, the price must be reduced, not just on the extra unit but on all the units before. It is actually possible for the total revenue to fall because of the price reductions on the earlier units.

Price $	Output $	Total revenue $
10	0	0
9	1	9
8	2	16
7	3	21
6	4	24
5	5	25
4	6	24
3	7	21

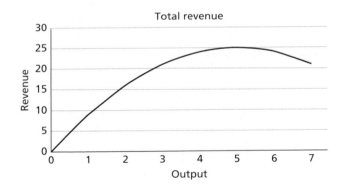

Total revenue

Objectives of firms

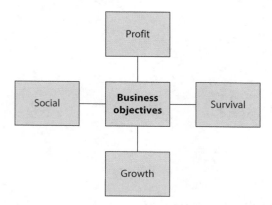

Profit maximisation occurs when there is the biggest positive difference possible between total revenue and total costs. Firms may want to earn profit to:

- reward their owners
- use as a source of funds.

Other business objectives may be:

- social – to provide a service for society, e.g. heath service
- survival – when starting out or when struggling, a business may be more interested in surviving even if profits are low; it may lower price to and try and keep sales going
- growth – a business may invest in expansion; this investment may reduce profits but lead to growth and potentially more profits in the long term.

Quick test

1. State the equation to calculate profit.
2. Define 'fixed costs'.
3. Define 'variable costs'.
4. What is the difference between total cost and average cost?
5. State **two** uses of profit.

Market structure

Competitive markets

The competitiveness of a market will depend on how many firms there are within it and their relative size. A competitive market will have many firms of a similar size competing for customers. This means there is an incentive to get better and to be better than your competitors in order to win sales. Businesses will be constantly trying to develop a better product to attract customers away from their rivals. They will also be trying to be as efficient as they can as this will allow them to lower prices to increase the quantity demanded. Competitive forces should, therefore, be good for customers.

It should lead to:

- more innovation as businesses try to improve what they offer (their products) or the processes they use to produce and deliver their products
- lower prices for consumers as businesses try to become more efficient to allow them to cut prices lower than their competitors
- better quality products for consumers as businesses try to attract customers
- a better quality service.

In competitive markets, each firm will have to try harder to attract and keep customers. If they do not, then existing firms or new firms will take their customers from them.

Competitive markets mean customers have choice and this puts pressure on firms to deliver high quality at a relatively low price.

Monopoly markets

Monopoly power exists when one firm dominates a market and has a high **market share**, i.e. the sales of the firm are a high percentage of the total market sales. In a pure monopoly, there is only one firm selling in the market, i.e the market share of the business is 100%. In reality when one business has a market share of around 25% or more, this is regarded by governments as a monopoly because it is so dominant.

Monopolies are carefully watched by governments because they are potentially so powerful. Monopolies mean customers have limited (if any) choice. This means the monopoly can be a price maker (rather than a price taker which is what happens in competitive markets because firms have to watch what others firms charge and take their price from this). The danger is that monopolies can abuse their power and push up prices to 'exploit' the customer who has no choice. The monopolist may also lack much incentive to innovate because there is no pressure to do so. There is no competition from others so they can carry on as they are and the service could be poor for customers. Governments can regulate monopolies to ensure that the price they charge is fair and that the service they provide is appropriate.

> **You must be able to:**
> - explain the benefits of competition
> - understand what a monopoly is
> - explain the potential problems of monopoly power
> - explain the potential benefits of monopoly power.

> **Revision tip**
>
> Remember, there are arguments for and against monopolies. Do not assume they only have a negative impact on the economy.

However it should not be assumed that monopolies are always bad. For example, the business may be a monopoly because it is innovative:

- its monopoly power may come from developing new products and processes better than competitors
- the quality of the product and service may be outstanding, which is why the business dominates the market
- the profits the monopolist makes may encourage more businesses to be innovative to try and replace this firm, i.e. the dominance of one firm encourages others to innovate
- having a monopoly may mean resources are not wasted by having several firms doing exactly the same thing
- the monopolist may be more efficient and gain more internal economies of scale.

This is why monopolies are not assumed to be bad – each case is usually investigated by the government to assess on its own merits. In fact monopolies are sometimes encouraged by governments. For example, when someone invents a new product or process, they can usually be granted a patent by a government which prevents others copying it for a number of years. This is intended to encourage innovation in an economy.

Barriers to entry

A monopoly occurs because of barriers to entry. These prevent other forms coming into a market. They include:

- legal protection by the government, e.g. a patent or the protection of a domestic industry from foreign competition
- state provision, e.g. the government takes control of the industry and becomes the only provider
- brand loyalty achieved through marketing meaning that others cannot gain customers
- technological advantages that others do not know how to copy
- control over resources, e.g. control over natural resources
- cost advantages, e.g. efficient production processes that enable the business to produce at much lower unit costs and sell at much lower prices than others can.

Argument against monopolies	Argument for monopolies
charges a higher price to consumers than in competitive market	may use the high profits to invest in research and development, which may lead to innovation over time – it could lead to better products and lower costs than a competitive market
may provide poor quality goods / services because customers have no choice	may encourage other firms to be more innovative to remove the monopoly
may be little incentive to innovate or improve because it dominates a market and there is a lack of competition	may mean there is a not a waste of resources, e.g. with two business providing the same service

Quick test

1. State **two** possible benefits for consumers of a competitive market.
2. What is meant by 'market share'?
3. Explain what is meant by 'monopoly power'.
4. Give **one** reason why monopolies may not be in the public interest.
5. Give **one** reason why monopolies may be in the public interest.

Exam-style practice questions

1. Which statement is **true**? [1]

   a) fixed costs divided by revenue equals total costs

   b) fixed costs do not change with output

   c) fixed costs never change

   d) fixed costs plus average costs equal total costs

2. Prices tend to be lower in a competitive industry than in a monopoly. Why is this? [1]

   a) a monopoly has less influence on the market

   b) competitive industry has more economies of scale

   c) new firms are free to enter the competitive industry

   d) profits are lower in a monopoly

3. Which is **most** likely to make consumers save more? [1]

   a) a belief that the prices of goods and services will rise in the future

   b) an increase in the individual's wish to enjoy higher consumption immediately

   c) lower interest rates paid by banks

   d) worries that they will lose their jobs and income will fall in the future

4. Wages are **most** likely to be low in industries where [1]

   a) there is an excess supply of labour.

   b) the work is dangerous.

   c) workers are paid on a monthly basis.

   d) workers need several years of training.

5. A trade union is negotiating a wage rise for its members.
   What is likely to increase the chance of the wage rise being granted? [1]

   a) the economy is beginning to enter a recession

   b) the government has made strike action illegal

   c) the product the business produces has many substitutes

   d) wages are a small part of the company's costs

6 A tyre manufacturer expands by taking over a rubber plantation.
What is this an example of? [1]

a) backward vertical integration

b) diversifying integration

c) forward vertical integration

d) horizontal integration

7 **Google**

In 2017, the internet giant, Google, was fined \$2.7 billion by the European Union's (EU) Competition Commission. The Commission investigated the company for abusing its monopoly power and found that Google was dominant in general internet search markets in Europe with a market share of about 90%.

The Commission stated that when people were searching for items, Google would promote its own shopping comparison sites and set these out at the top of the search results without people knowing they were Google. The company had to stop doing this or face more fines.

A spokesperson said: 'Google has come up with many innovative products and services that have made a difference to our lives. That's a good thing. But Google's strategy for its comparison shopping service wasn't just about attracting customers by making its product better than those of its rivals. Instead, Google abused its market dominance as a search engine by promoting its own comparison shopping service in its search results, and demoting those of competitors.

What Google has done is illegal under the EU rules to control monopoly behaviour. It denied other companies the chance to compete on their merits and to innovate. And most importantly, it denied European consumers a genuine choice of services and the full benefits of innovation.'

Google immediately rejected the Commission's findings, and said it would appeal.

Google's revenue in 2016 was around \$89 billion. The company has over \$52 billion in cash, which is held abroad because of the taxes it would have to pay if the money was brought back to the US.

Whilst being a monopoly is not in itself illegal, under EU law, companies that are dominant are not allowed to abuse their position by restricting competition. On the back of the finding that Google is the dominant player in the European search engine market, the EU regulator is further investigating how else the company may have abused its position, specifically in its provision of maps, images and information on local services.

a) What is meant by 'market share'? [2]

b) Define 'a monopoly'. [2]

c) Explain why Google was investigated by the Competition Commission. [4]

d) Calculate Google's fine as a percentage of its revenue in 2016. [2]

e) Explain why Google might want to become a monopoly. [4]

f) Analyse how Google might have achieved its monopoly position. [4]

g) Discuss whether taxing monopolies is a good way to ensure they behave in the public interest. [6]

h) Discuss whether monopolies are bad for consumers. [6]

8 Nearly 80% of employees in the United Arab Emirates work in the service sector. The region has attracted many large firms in industries such as tourism and finance and energy. Operating on a large scale may give these firms lower unit costs, helping them to be globally competitive. However, the region also has many startups and small businesses. Small and medium-sized enterprises account for around 40% of all jobs and income in the region.

a) Define tertiary sector. [2]

b) Explain how the size of a business may be measured. [4]

c) Analyse the benefits small firms can bring to an economy. [6]

d) Discuss whether large firms inevitably have lower unit costs than smaller firms. [8]

9 The trade union representing thousands of low-paid production workers employed by the BBC in the UK recently called for a minimum salary of $26 000. BECTU – the Broadcasting, Entertainment, Cinematograph and Theatre Union – said it was 'unjustifiable' for some in the organisation to be earning more than $198 000 when thousands of engineers, technical and other production staff were paid much less than that amount. The minimum wage in the UK is around $9.90 per hour.

a) Identify three factors that may determine an individual's choice of occupation. [2]

b) Explain why the minimum wage legislation in the UK may not have an effect on the earnings of most BBC staff. [4]

c) Analyse the factors that determine how much someone earns. [6]

d) Discuss whether membership of a trade union will always benefit a worker. [8]

The role and macroeconomic aims of government

Government and its role

The **government** is:

- a producer of goods and services in an economy, e.g. a government may provide some of the transport in a country, education, healthcare, emergency services and defence
- an employer of workers, such as nurses, doctors, teachers, and police and military personnel.

Organisations that are owned by the government are part of the **public sector.** The size of the public sector varies from country to country, e.g. it is relatively large in China and relatively small in the USA.

A government will influence:

- the local economy – local government is often responsible for the provision of local services, such as libraries, roads and waste collection
- the national economy – government policies (actions taken by government) will affect how easy it to set up in business, demand levels, the growth of the economy, and the costs and prices of factors of production
- the international economy – government policies will influence the trade between one country and another, which will affect growth in the world economy.

The government can influence the **private sector** by:

- **nationalisation**, i.e. taking over the provision of a good or service
- **privatisation**, i.e. selling public sector assets to the private sector
- **taxation**, e.g. **indirect taxes** on goods and services (paid when the item is bought) or **direct taxes** on income and profits (taken directly from earnings)
- **subsidies**, e.g. cash payments or tax reductions for producers
- **regulation**, e.g. laws influencing the amount produced, how it is produced, how people are employed, how products are marketed.

> You must be able to:
> - understand the role of government in the public and private sectors
> - explain what is meant by the macroeconomic objectives
> - explain how these objectives may complement each other or conflict with each other.

The macroeconomic aims of government

A government **objective** is a target that it sets for the economy as a whole.

Government macroeconomic objectives include:

Economic growth

Economic growth is shown by an increase in national income. Generally the government will want economic growth so that its citizens are earning more. If income increases and the population remains the same, the income per person rises. Higher income per person is usually associated with a higher standard of living.

Full employment

Full employment means that all those willing and able to work at the given real wage are in work. The government will want low levels of unemployment as it is a waste of resources (inefficient) and socially undesirable. If people are working, it should help economic growth and give people a better standard of living.

Price stability

If prices are changing unpredictably, it is difficult for firms to plan investment or for households to plan how much they will spend and how much they need to save. Stable prices enable better planning and give businesses and households more confidence in the government's control of the economy.

Balance of payments stability

The **balance of payments** position measures the financial transactions between one country and the rest of the world. If a country is buying in heavily from abroad, it suggests its businesses are uncompetitive. If it is selling far more abroad than it is buying in, other governments may want to take action to protect their own industries. A government will aim for a stable trade position in terms of **exports** and **imports**.

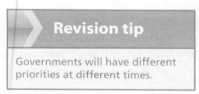

Revision tip

Governments will have different priorities at different times.

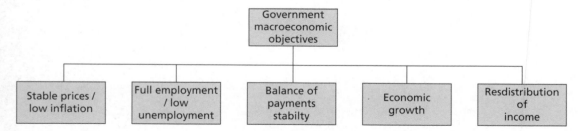

Other macroeconomic objectives of government may relate to:

* redistribution of income, e.g. to reduce inequality and poverty
* environmental targets, e.g. reducing carbon emissions and reducing global warming.

Possible conflicts between macroeconomic aims

Some macroeconomic objectives may work well together, for example:

- economic growth can help create jobs and reduce unemployment
- stable prices may make trade more appealing and help a country's trade position.

However, some macroeconomic objectives may conflict with each other, for example:

- increased spending to reduce unemployment may lead to higher prices
- economic growth may lead to more spending on imports, which may worsen the trade position
- economic growth may have negative environmental effects
- higher taxes on high income earners (to make the distribution of income more even) may deter entrepreneurs and lead to slower economic growth.

Quick test

1. What is meant by 'economic growth'?
2. Why may economic growth be an objective of government?
3. Why does a government want low unemployment?
4. What is the purpose of the balance of payments?
5. What is the 'public sector'?

Fiscal policy

Fiscal policy and government spending

Fiscal policy involves changes to government spending and the taxation and benefits system to influence the economy.

Government spending may be at a national or local government level and may be on areas such as defence, transport, healthcare, education and justice.

The government budget position

The **budget position** is the difference between government spending and government revenue in a given period, usually a year.

- A **budget deficit** occurs when government revenue is less than government spending.
- A **budget surplus** occurs when government revenue is more than government spending.

Taxation

Taxation is a charge made by the government (e.g. on goods and services), which:

- raises the revenue of the government
- can be used to influence behavior, e.g. encourage consumers to use more environmentally-friendly energy.

Taxation can take the form of:

- **direct tax** – taken directly from earnings, e.g. income tax and corporation tax (a tax charged on profits)
- **indirect tax** – charged when items are bought, e.g. value added tax (VAT).

Progressive taxation

- The average rate of tax increases as income increases. This occurs when the marginal rate of tax gets higher as earnings increase. The higher proportion of extra tax being paid pulls up the average rate of taxation.

Regressive taxation

The average rate of tax decreases as income increases. This occurs when the marginal rate of tax gets lower as earnings increase. The lower proportion of extra tax being paid pulls down the average rate of taxation.

> **Revision tip**
>
> Remember, if the government has a deficit, it is spending more than it earns, which should boost demand.

Proportional taxation

The average rate of tax stays the same regardless of income. This occurs when the marginal rate of tax remains constant as earnings increase.

Types of taxation system

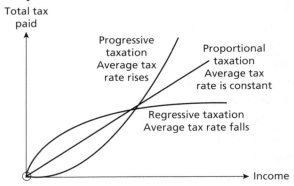

Principles of taxation

A good tax system should be:

- easy to administer
- cost effective – it should not be too expensive to collect the taxes or to monitor whether people and businesses are paying the right amount of tax
- fair – it must treat people in the same financial situation in the same way
- easy to understand – people need to know what they are supposed to pay.

Impact of taxation

Taxation can have an impact on different economic agents:

- consumers – tax may reduce earnings (e.g. income tax), reduce **wealth** (e.g. inheritance tax) and increase the **cost of living** (e.g. VAT)
- employees – the benefits and tax system will affect the incentive to work
- firms – tax may reduce profits (e.g. corporation tax), increase costs (e.g. taxes on imported goods) and affect selling price (e.g. VAT)
- government – tax may be used to reduce consumption (e.g. tobacco) or raise revenue (e.g. income tax).

Taxation can affect:

- the **demand** in the economy, e.g. higher income tax will reduce disposable incomes (income after tax), which is likely to reduce consumption spending; higher corporation tax may affect the funds firms have for investment and reduce spending on capital goods
- the **supply** in the economy, e.g. higher income tax may reduce the incentive for employees to work, which will reduce the labour force and output in the economy; tax incentives may encourage investment, which can increase productivity and supply in the long run.

Revision tip

The effect of a change in the taxation rate will depend on which tax it is, e.g. income tax affects households directly, whereas corporation tax affects firms.

It is also important to consider the system as a whole. For example, for income tax, you need to consider the different levels of income at which different tax rates are applied.

Taxation and macroeconomic objectives

Macroeconomic objectives	Taxation can...
economic growth	• affect the supply of resources, e.g. by affecting the incentive to invest and work
full employment	• affect the demand in the economy, e.g. through income tax and corporation tax, which can affect the demand for jobs
price stability	• affect costs (indirect taxes) and, therefore, prices • affect the level of demand, which can also affect prices
balance of payments stability	• be placed on goods and services from abroad, which will affect spending on overseas products

Quick test

1. What is meant by 'fiscal policy'?
2. The rate of tax increases as income increases. What type of tax system is this?
3. Explain the difference between a direct tax and an indirect tax.
4. What is meant by a 'budget deficit'?
5. State **three** areas of government spending.

Monetary policy

Monetary policy measures

Monetary policy involves the central bank taking action to influence interest rates, the supply of money and the **exchange rate** to affect the economy.

The **interest rate** is the cost of borrowing money (and the reward for saving). By changing the interest rate, the central bank changes the incentive for households and firms to save and spend. This influences spending in the economy.

A higher interest rate may:

- decrease consumption by discouraging households to borrow (because it is more expensive to do so) – the effect depends on how sensitive borrowing is to interest rates
- decrease investment by discouraging businesses to borrow (because it is more expensive to do so) – the effect depends on how sensitive borrowing is to interest rates
- decrease exports by increasing the demand to save in the country (because of the higher returns) – this will increase demand for the currency, which is likely to increase its value; a higher exchange rate makes exports more expensive in foreign currency, which is likely to decrease the sale of exports and export spending.

A lower interest rate may:

- increase consumption by encouraging households to borrow (because it is cheap to do so)
- increase investment by encouraging businesses to borrow (because it is cheap to do so)
- increase exports by reducing demand to save in the country (because of the lower returns) – this will reduce demand for the currency, which is likely to lower its value; a lower exchange rate makes exports cheaper in foreign currency, which is likely to increase the sale of exports and export spending.

You must be able to:
- explain what is meant by 'monetary policy'
- understand what is meant by the 'interest rate'
- explain the effect of changes in the interest rate on households, firms and the economy
- explain the effects of changes in the interest rate on macroeconomic objectives.

> **Revision tip**
>
> The interest rate is the reward to savers and the cost of borrowing. The effect will be different on these different groups. Higher interest rates may be welcomed by savers but not by borrowers.

Effects of monetary policy on macroeconomic objectives

Macroeconomic objective	Monetary policy
economic growth	interest rates can affect the level of investment in an economy
full employment	interest rates can affect borrowing and spending by households and firms and, therefore, demand for goods and services and jobs
price stability	interest rates will affect demand; increases in demand are likely to pull up prices
balance of payments stability	interest rates will affect the incentive to save within a country – higher interest rates will affect the demand for its currency and, therefore, the price of its currency (exchange rate); higher interest rates tend to increase the value of the exchange rate, which means exports are more expensive in foreign currency and, therefore, fall

Quick test

1. What is meant by 'monetary policy'?
2. What is meant by an 'interest rate'?
3. Explain how a low interest rate may affect investment in an economy.
4. Explain how a low interest rate may affect consumption in an economy.
5. Explain how a high interest rate may affect the exchange rate of an economy.

Supply-side policy

Supply-side policy measures

Supply-side policies aim to improve the quantity and quality of the factors of production in an economy to increase its productive potential. This should increase the long-term supply of goods and services in an economy. A policy is a deliberate set of actions taken by the government to bring about an improvement in supply-side conditions.

Supply-sides policies aim to shift the supply outwards by increasing the quantity and / or quality of resources. They increase the amount produced at each and every price level.

An increase in the long-run supply in the economy can lead to:

- economic growth and more output
- more employment
- lower prices, which can increase the international competitiveness of a country.

Supply-side policies include intervention by the government:

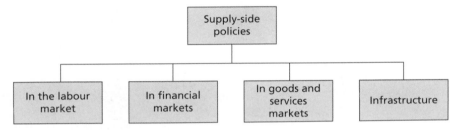

The labour market

Supply-side policies in the labour market include:

- reducing welfare benefits to provide a greater incentive to work
- providing more training to employees to increase their skills and to provide the skills needed in the modern economy
- reducing direct taxation to provide greater incentive to work
- providing more information to employees so they know what jobs are available
- helping employees relocate to where the jobs are (e.g. helping with housing costs)
- improving healthcare so that employees are off work less due to illness
- changing legislation to reduce trade union power.

The financial markets

Supply-side policies in the financial markets include:

- helping businesses to have easier access to finance
- providing cheaper finance to enable businesses to invest and grow.

Goods and services markets

Supply-side policies in goods and services markets include:

- reducing startup bureaucracy to encourage entrepreneurs
- encouraging investment in research and development and innovation
- subsidising investment in some industries
- protecting infant industries to help their development

- encouraging more competition to generate more innovation and research, e.g. governments may limit takeovers and mergers if they lead to monopoly power.

Infrastructure

Supply-side policies in relation to infrastructure include:

- improving the number of business and firms with fast broadband
- improving the transport system
- improving broadband access and the speed of internet access.

The effects of supply-side policy measures on macroeconomic aims

Supply-side policies can increase the long-run supply. An increase in supply can lead to:

- less unemployment
- lower prices
- economic growth.

Supply-side improvements do not only come through the government. They also come from the private sector, e.g. in terms of innovation and productivity gains.

Productivity may be increased through:

- better training
- better management
- investment in capital and technology.

Innovation may be encouraged by:

- a stable business environment
- tax incentives for businesses who invest
- efforts to link innovators and investors (e.g. universities and business).

Revision tip

Sometimes the focus of government policy may be supply-side. At other times, a government may think the key issue is to raise aggregate demand.

Macroeconomic objective	Supply-side policies...
economic growth	• can increase supply leading to economic growth
full employment	• can provide more incentive to work • can increase the level of full employment
price stability	• can increase supply and, therefore, lower prices
balance of payments stability	• can improve supply and, therefore, increase exports

Quick test

1. What is meant by 'supply-side policies'?
2. State **two** possible supply-side policies for the labour market.
3. State **one** possible supply-side policy for the infrastructure.
4. State **one** possible example of supply-side policies in relation to industries.
5. State **one** possible example of supply-side policies in relation to financial markets.

Economic growth

Measurement of economic growth

Economic growth occurs when there is an increase in national income over time, e.g. 2% annual growth means national income has increased by 2% over the year.

Gross domestic product (GDP) is the value of all the income generated in an economy over a year. Real GDP is the value of GDP adjusted for inflation, e.g. if national income grows by 2% but, over the same period, prices have increased by 2% as well, the real GDP has not changed.

$$\textbf{Real GDP per head} \text{ (or per capita)} = \frac{\text{Real GDP}}{\text{population}}$$

If real GDP stays the same and the population increases, the real GDP per head would fall.

Real GDP per head is the most common measure of **standard of living** in a country. It is the average income per person.

Economic growth may be shown by:

- an increase in the productive potential of the economy – an outward shift of the production possibility curve
- a movement towards full employment – a movement from within the PPC onto the curve; this is actual growth, but involves getting the economy up to its potential output and removing a negative output gap rather than increasing its productive potential.

Economic growth

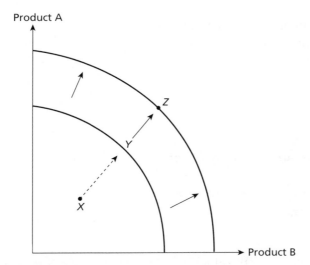

The movement from *X* to *Y* is an increase in output, but it is reducing inefficiency and restoring the economy to its productive capacity. The movement from *Y* to *Z* represents growth in the productive capacity of the economy – the PPC has shifted outwards.

You must be able to:
- define 'economic growth'
- explain how economic growth is measured
- explain why economic growth is a government objective
- understand the causes of economic growth
- understand the stages of the economic cycle.

> **Revision tip**
>
> Real GDP per head only shows an average. When considering the standard of living in a country, it is important to consider how the income was distributed.

> **Revision tip**
>
> Remember, there is a difference between an increase in national income that is achieved by using existing resources more efficiently, and an increase in national income that is due to an increase in the quantity or quality of the factors of production.

The economic (or business or trade) cycle

The **economic (business or trade) cycle** describes the growth pattern of an economy's income over time. Typically an economy goes through the following stages:

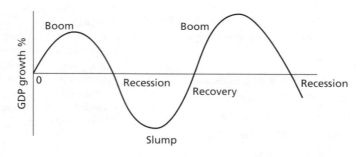

Boom

A **boom** occurs when output is growing faster than the average trend rate. In a boom there is usually:

- a high level of consumption, which increases demand and can pull up prices
- an increase in investment as businesses invest in extra capacity
- low levels of unemployment
- high spending on imports due to higher incomes
- higher tax revenue for the government due to higher incomes, profits and spending.

Slowdown

A **slowdown** occurs when the rate of income growth slows down, but the economy is still growing.

Recession

A **recession** occurs when there is a fall in national income (GDP) for two consecutive quarters (i.e. six months). A recession is associated with:

- lower profits
- less upward pressure on prices
- greater capacity
- less employment
- less investment
- less tax revenue for the government as there are lower profits and incomes
- less confidence by consumers, which can reduce spending further
- less spending on imports as there is less income.

Slump

A **slump** is a sustained and major recession leading to a significant fall in output. A **depression** occurs when there is a fall in real GDP of more than 10% from the peak of the economic cycle to its lowest point of recession.

Recovery

A **recovery** occurs when real GDP picks up from the low point of the recession. This may be because business and household confidence starts to improve, leading to more spending and investment. It may also be due to government policies to promote a recovery, such as:

- lower interest rates to encourage borrowing
- expansionist spending on goods and services by the government
- lower taxation by the government to encourage investment and spending.

Economic growth can lead to:

- more income for households
- greater consumer confidence, which can lead to more spending and act as an incentive for firms to invest
- more tax revenue for governments (e.g. from taxes on spending and profits) and less spending on benefits, as there will be fewer people unemployed, which means the budget position should improve
- higher profits for businesses, enabling more investment in innovation, research and development, which enables future economic growth.

The causes of economic growth include:

- an increase in the amount of capital in an economy, enabling more to be produced
- an increase in the working population or the quality of labour
- improvements in technology
- increased demand for exports
- government policies that encourage innovation and startup businesses and remove barriers to setting up and running a business.

Quick test

1. What is meant by 'GDP'?
2. What is meant by 'real GDP'?
3. What is meant by a 'recession'?
4. State **two** ways in which a government may stimulate economic growth.
5. How would economic growth be shown on a production possibility curve?

Employment and unemployment

Changing patterns and levels of employment

Employment is the number of people in work. The **pattern of employment** is the types of jobs that people do. Typically, economies begin with many people working in the primary sector (e.g. in North Korea). Over time, more people tend to move into manufacturing in the secondary sector (e.g. in China). With further economic growth, more developed economies tend to have a large tertiary sector (e.g. in the UK).

Other changes in employment patterns may include:

- changes to the number of women in the workforce
- changes to the age at which people tend to retire (length of time worked)
- shifts between the private and public sectors, e.g. if the government takes less responsibility for the provision of goods and services, the public sector declines and, as more labour moves into it, the private sector grows.

The **level of unemployment** measures the number of people who are willing and able to work but are not employed at the given wage rate at a given moment in time.

The **unemployment rate** is the number of people unemployed as a percentage of the total workforce.

$$\text{Unemployment rate (\%)} = \frac{\text{number of people unemployed}}{\text{number of people in workforce}} \times 100$$

Unemployment can be measured by:

- the **claimant count** – the number of people entitled to claim unemployment benefit over a given time period
- a **labour force survey** – a survey that measures the number of people who say they are looking for work at the given real wage rate.

Causes and types of unemployment

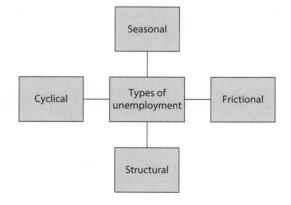

Seasonal unemployment

People are unemployed because of the time of year, e.g. they worked on fruit farms in the summer and are unemployed in the winter.

You must be able to:

- define 'employment' and 'unemployment'
- understand what is meant by changing patterns of employment
- understand how unemployment is measured
- distinguish between the unemployment level and the unemployment rate
- understand different causes of unemployment
- explain the policies a government may adopt to reduce unemployment.

> **Revision tip**
>
> The level of unemployment is measured as the number of people. The unemployment rate is a percentage of the labour force.

Frictional unemployment

People are between jobs, e.g. someone has left one job and is waiting before starting another job. As long as there is a continual flow into and out of work, frictional unemployment is not necessarily a concern.

Structural unemployment

The competitiveness of different parts of an economy change, e.g. a country may become less competitive in shipbuilding but more competitive in software design. People are made unemployed in shipbuilding, but may not be able to retrain to become software designers due to occupational or geographical immobility.

Cyclical (demand deficient) unemployment

There is a lack of **aggregate demand** in the economy. With less demand for products, there is less demand for labour, which causes unemployment.

Consequences of unemployment

The private costs of unemployment (for the individual) include:

* lower income
* possible loss of self-esteem.

The social costs of unemployment include:

* a waste of resources, which means output and growth in the economy is less than it could be
* possible social divisions (between the employed and unemployed)
* a possible increase in crime.

Policies to reduce unemployment

The best way for a government to reduce unemployment depends on the underlying cause. For example, a government may:

* increase aggregate demand to create jobs for those who are cyclically unemployed
* retrain workers to reduce structural unemployment
* reduce unemployment benefits and make accepting a job more financially attractive (e.g. by reducing income tax) to reduce frictional unemployment.

Revision tip

For the government to reduce unemployment, it needs to know what is causing it.

Quick test

1. State **two** social problems caused by unemployment.
2. Define 'structural unemployment'.
3. State **one** way of reducing cyclical unemployment.
4. State **one** way of reducing structural unemployment.
5. What is the difference between level of unemployment and unemployment rate as measures?

Inflation and deflation

Measurement of inflation

Inflation occurs when there is a sustained increase in the general price level over a period of time, e.g. if annual inflation is 2%, it means that prices in general increased by 2% over the last year.

Inflation measures the **cost of living**. This is a measure of changes in the average cost of buying a basket of different goods and services for a typical household.

Consumer Price Index (CPI)

The **Consumer Price Index (CPI)** is a **weighted price index** and is a common measure of inflation. The weights reflect the relative importance of different items in a typical household's shopping basket and come from the Family Expenditure Survey.

Examples

Category	Price index	Weighting	Price × weight
food	105	20	2100
alcohol & tobacco	108	5	540
clothing	95	15	1425
transport	110	14	1540
housing	105	20	2100
leisure services	102	8	816
household goods	94	12	1128
other items	110	6	660
		100	10309

In the example index above, food has a higher weighting than alcohol and tobacco, i.e. changes in the price of food will have a greater impact on the overall inflation rate.

$$\text{Price index} = \frac{\text{sum of (price} \times \text{weight)}}{\text{sum of weight}}$$

In this case, price index = $\frac{10309}{100}$ = 103.09. This is a 3.09% increase on the base year value of 100.

A fall in inflation

Inflation measures the rate of increase in prices. If inflation falls, prices are still increasing but at a slower rate, e.g. if inflation falls from 3% to 2%, the rate of increase in prices is slower, but there is still an increase.

Inflation 3% (Prices are growing by 3%)	Inflation 2% (Prices are still growing but by 2% not 3%)
Year 1	**Year 2**

Revision tip

Remember, the cost of living refers to the price of items in an economy. The standard of living measures how much real income (purchasing power) people have. The cost of living could be increasing but, if incomes are rising faster, the standard of living could rise.

Revision tip

The CPI measures inflation for the average household. If a household's spending patterns are different from the average then their inflation may be different from the official figures.

Revision tip

Lower inflation means that prices are increasing at a slower rate, not that they are falling.

Causes of inflation and policies to control it

There are two types of inflation:

Demand-pull inflation

An increase in demand can lead to higher prices. The impact on prices depends on the extent of the increase and how price inelastic supply is, e.g. supply becomes more price inelastic as the economy approaches full employment. Government may attempt to reduce **demand-pull inflation** by using deflationary policies to reduce demand, e.g. reducing government spending or increasing taxation rates. Demand-pull inflation is associated with high levels of demand, waiting lists, queues and shortages.

Cost-push inflation

An increase in costs can lead to higher prices, e.g. an increase in energy costs can push up the costs of production. Supply moves inwards. Government may attempt to reduce **cost-push inflation** by controlling wage increases (through income policies) or by intervening to increase the value of the exchange rate to reduce import prices. Cost-push inflation is associated with higher prices, lower levels of output and higher levels of unemployment.

Consequences of inflation

Inflation can affect consumers, firms, government, workers and society.

Inflation can create uncertainty – businesses do not know how much their resources will cost and what they will be selling their products for, which can deter investment. It can also affect:

*   **menu costs**, as businesses have to change their prices regularly
*   **shoe leather costs** (administrative costs), as businesses, workers and households look for the best returns to compensate for inflation.

Households may have less real income depending on their ability to increase nominal earnings in line with inflation. Workers with relatively little bargaining power, such as the unemployed and pensioners, are likely to be worse off in real terms. This can lead to more inequality in society.

Households may also find their savings have fallen in real terms because they can buy less (unless the return they are earning is greater than inflation).

If inflation is higher than abroad then, assuming the exchange rate is unaltered, a country's exports will decline because they are relatively expensive and uncompetitive. This may affect government policy.

Tax revenue for the government may increase as, with more nominal income, people pay more taxes, e.g. if your income rises 3% and inflation is 3%, you are not better off in real terms but may be in a higher tax bracket and have to pay a higher tax rate. This is called **fiscal drag**.

Deflation

Deflation occurs when there is a sustained fall in the general price level over a given period. It means there is a negative inflation rate. This can be caused by a fall in demand.

If prices are falling:

- consumers and businesses may decide to save and spend later when prices are lower, which can lead to a further decrease in demand, creating a deflationary spiral
- the real value of a debt increases, which can reduce consumer and business confidence and spending
- profit margins may fall, leading to efforts to reduce costs, such as job losses.

Revision tip

To reduce inflation, the cause has to be known. The right policy depends on the underlying cause.

Quick test

1. Define 'inflation'.
2. What is meant by 'demand-pull inflation'?
3. What is meant by 'cost-push inflation'?
4. State **two** effects of inflation on firms.
5. State **one** effect of deflation on firms.

Chapter 4
Government
and
macroeconomy

Exam-style practice questions

1. Economic growth can be defined as [1]

   a) an increase in a country's exports.

   b) an increase in a country's population.

   c) an increase in the productive capacity of an economy.

   d) a reduction in inflation.

2. What effect is a decrease in interest rates likely to have on consumers and firms? [1]

   a) borrow less, invest less

   b) borrow less, invest more

   c) save less, invest less

   d) save less, invest more

3. When may high inflation and low interest rates **most** worry consumers? [1]

   a) when a consumer has a pension that is linked to the consumer price index

   b) when a consumer pays a fixed rent for their accommodation

   c) when a consumer relies on his or her savings

   d) when a consumer wants to buy a product on credit

4. Which **best** describes unemployment caused by the decline of an industry due to technological change? [1]

   a) CPI unemployment

   b) frictional unemployment

   c) seasonal unemployment

   d) structural unemployment

5. Which is an inevitable consequence of deflation? [1]

   a) a fall in exports

   b) a fall in the standard of living

   c) an increase in the cost of living

   d) an increase in the real value of money

6. Which is a supply-side policy likely to promote economic growth? [1]

   a) an increase in benefit payments

   b) an increase in the funding of training

   c) an increase in the rate of corporation tax

   d) an increase in the rate of income tax

7 **The South African budget deficit**

In 2017, the South African government decided to raise taxes to improve the government's budget position. The finance minister said that the Treasury would need to raise an extra R28 billion ($2.1 billion) in taxes to help meet the budget deficit target for the year of 3.1% of GDP. The shortfall between revenue and spending was very noticeable because the economy was expected to grow by only about 1.3% that year, making the deficit a larger percentage of national income.

To reduce the deficit, the Treasury cut spending in many areas. It also announced a top income tax rate of 45% for people earning more than R1.5 million. The tax increases were aimed at higher income earners to make the system more progressive. The government also raised fuel taxes. However, it decided not to increase VAT, as this was felt to be too politically unpopular.

In preceding years, the South African government had been good at maintaining a healthy budget position. This allowed it to borrow from domestic and international lenders. However, growth had been slow and unemployment and poverty were high. South Africa's unemployment rate hit a 12-year high in 2016, at 27.3% in the third quarter of the year. The unemployment rate was even higher among youths, close to 50%.

South Africa also has one of the highest inequality rates in the world. The poorest 20% of the South African population consume less than 3% of total expenditure, while the wealthiest 20% consume 65%. The government knows it has to reduce inequality and ensure black South Africans fully share in expanded job and wealth creation, while boosting incomes for everyone.

Fig. 1: South African government budget

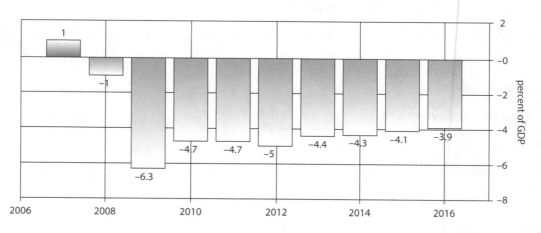

a) What is meant by 'GDP'? [2]

b) South Africa has a budget deficit. Explain what is meant by a 'budget deficit'. [2]

c) Explain what is meant by a 'progressive tax system'. [2]

d) Explain **two** possible reasons why South Africa has a budget deficit. [4]

e) Explain **two** possible causes of inequality in South Africa. [4]

f) Explain **two** reasons why the South African government might have taxed fuel. [4]

g) Discuss the possible consequences of high unemployment in South Africa. [6]

h) Discuss how the South African government may try to increase economic growth in the country. [6]

8 Gambia has a very high unemployment rate and this has increased in recent years with lower demand in the economy. Lower demand means output is below its potential level. Tourism normally brings in about 20% of Gambia's GDP, but the country suffered in 2014 from tourists' fears of the Ebola virus in neighbouring West African countries. The economy has also suffered from a lack of investment due to high interest rates. The government is committed to reducing unemployment and is considering whether demand or supply-side policies are better.

a) Define the 'potential output' of an economy.   [2]

b) Explain the consequences of high unemployment.   [4]

c) Analyse the different causes of unemployment that could exist in an economy.   [6]

d) Discuss the best way for a government to reduce unemployment in its economy.   [8]

9 The economic policy of the prime minister Mr Abe in Japan was called the 'three arrows'. It involves a stimulus from monetary policy, fiscal policy and supply-side policies in areas of the economy, such as the labour market. These were aimed at helping economic growth and reducing unemployment. However, by 2017, there were calls for greater spending by the government to increase demand. Some advisers said there had not been a fiscal policy boost as the government had raised taxes to raise revenue and reduce the budget deficit.

a) Define 'budget deficit'.   [2]

b) Explain how supply-side policies in the labour market might reduce unemployment.   [4]

c) Analyse how changes in fiscal policy can affect economic growth.   [6]

d) Discuss whether an increase in spending or a reduction in tax is the better way of reducing unemployment.   [8]

Living standards

Real national income per capita

The **standard of living** in a country is usually measured by **real GDP per head**.

Real GDP is the value of **gross national income (GNI)** after it has been adjusted to take account of inflation. For example:

- if income increases by 3% but prices increase by 3%, in real terms you are no better off – real GDP remains the same
- if income increases by 5% and prices increase by 3%, real GDP has increased by 2%.

Real GDP per capita measures the average income per person.

$$\text{Real GDP per capita} = \frac{\text{real GDP}}{\text{population}}$$

Therefore, the standard of living between countries may vary according to:

- the size of national income
- the population size.

There are problems with real income per capita as a measure of the standard of living:

- It does not take into account accumulated wealth and assets.
- It does not take account of the quality of goods and services – over time, the price of products (e.g. consumer electronics) and, therefore, income may fall even though quality may be increasing.
- It does not take into account quality of life, e.g. how many hours were worked for the income.
- It does not take account of the **income distribution** – there could be major income inequality within the economy.
- It does not account for the value of unpaid work and trade, e.g. improvements made by the owners to their homes are not counted, whereas improvements made by paid tradespeople are. Similarly, it does not include anything traded through **barter**, because it has not been sold for a price.
- It does not account for undeclared activity (the 'shadow economy') – in some economies, there is a significant amount of buying and selling that goes unreported to avoid taxes.

To increase living standards as measured by real national income per capita, a government will want to increase economic growth. It may do this through supply-side policies to increase the amount that the economy can produce, e.g. invest in infrastructure, encourage innovation and provide more incentive to work.

> You must be able to:
> - explain what is meant by 'the standard of living' and how to measure it
> - describe why some countries are classified as 'developed' and others are not
> - discuss differences in standards of living within countries and between different countries.

Comparing incomes between countries

Differences in income between countries may be due to:

- the productivity of the workforce – this will depend on skills and training and the quality and quantity of resources it has to work with
- the size and structure of the population
- the quality of the education sector
- the amount of investment in capital
- the quality of the healthcare system – if the workforce is healthier, it may be more productive
- access to export markets and the ability to trade abroad
- the size of the primary, secondary and tertiary sectors – the secondary sector tends to become more productive with investment than the primary sector.

Comparing living standards and income distribution

The income per person will depend on what the overall income of the economy is and how many people there are. Over time, it will depend on the growth rates of both of these. For example, if the population is growing at 7% a year, the national income needs to grow at a similar rate for the income per person to stay constant.

The income distribution will depend on factors such as:

- the tax system and how progressive or regressive this is
- the benefits system
- how many people are of working age relative to those not working.

Measuring economic development

Measuring income may not be the best measure of economic development, i.e. the quality of a country's development and living standards may be better measured using a range of indicators. A country can have high income without being 'developed', e.g. if the income is earned by relatively few, the quality of life is poor and most people are not politically free.

The most common measurement of development is the **Human Development Index (HDI)**, published each year by the United Nations Development Programme. The index was developed to highlight the view that people and their capabilities are a better measure of the development of a country rather than economic growth alone. HDI is a summary measure of average achievement in a number of important dimensions, such as health, education and standard of living:

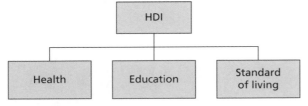

- The health dimension is measured by life expectancy at birth.
- Education is measured by the mean (average) years of schooling for adults (aged 15 and above) and expected years of schooling for children.
- The standard of living is measured by gross national income (GNI) per capita.

Human Development Index (HDI)

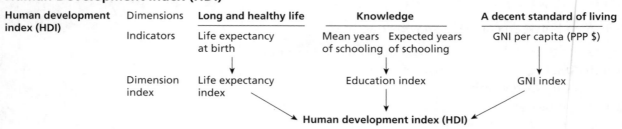

The HDI has a value of 0 to 1:

- 1 is total developed
- 0.8 and above is highly developed
- 0.5 to 0.8 is medium developed
- less than 0.5 is a low level of development.

Quick test

1. Define 'real GDP per head'?
2. What is meant by 'income distribution'?
3. State **two** limitations of real national income per capita as an indicator of the standard of living.
4. What is the difference between the standard of living and the cost of living?
5. Suggest **one** way a government may try to improve the country's standard of living.

Poverty

Poverty

Income is a flow concept. It shows the flow of earnings going to factors of production over a given period (usually a year), e.g. wages, rental income, interest from savings and profits. The flow of income earned in an economy over a year is measured by **gross domestic product (GDP)**.

Wealth is a stock concept. It shows the stock of assets (e.g. shares and property) a person, business or economy has at a given moment in time.

Income versus wealth

A person's wealth is everything they own minus what they owe. It may include their car, their apartment or house and their other possessions. These could have been bought at any time in their lives. Their income is their salary for that year. For example:

- if a person has a lot of assets but is not earning, they have high wealth and low income
- if a person has just started working and has a good income but relatively few assets, they have relatively low wealth and high income.

Income inequality measures how income is distributed within an economy.

Reducing the inequality within an economy (i.e. the difference between those with high and low incomes) is often an objective of government. This is deemed to be 'fair' but, in economic terms, it does not mean it is efficient. For example, a labour market may be economically efficient and lead to some people earning far more than others, which may not be seen as fair or good for society.

Very unequal incomes may lead to social unrest, as those with less become unhappy with those who have far more.

Absolute poverty

Absolute poverty is defined by the United Nations as 'a condition characterised by severe deprivation of basic human needs, including food, safe drinking water, sanitation facilities, health, shelter, education and information'. It depends not only on income, but also on access to services.

It occurs when incomes fall significantly below what is required to live a modest but adequate existence. Obviously, the decision about what is a modest and adequate existence is a value judgement, i.e. a matter of opinion, and society's views may change over time.

Relative poverty

Relative poverty occurs when an individual or household's income falls below a national average or median income.

Overall poverty

Overall poverty, as defined by the United Nations, takes various forms, including:

- a lack of income and a lack of productive resources to ensure sustainable livelihoods
- hunger and malnutrition
- ill health

- limited or lack of access to education and other basic services
- increased morbidity and mortality from illness
- homelessness and inadequate housing
- unsafe environments and social discrimination and exclusion.

It is also characterised by a lack of participation in decision-making and in civil and social issues.

Causes and effects of poverty

Poverty can lead to:

- a loss of status and income
- a decline in people's self-respect
- health issues
- a sense of social exclusion, which can create social conflict.

The main causes of poverty include:

- long-term unemployment (short-term unemployment, where people are simply between jobs, is less of an issue)
- low pay, e.g. due to discrimination or a lack of a minimum wage in the economy
- homelessness
- addiction, affecting health and employability.

Policies to alleviate poverty

Government policies to reduce poverty include:

- changes to the rate of taxation and benefits systems, e.g. reductions in the amount of tax paid by low earners (progressive taxation) and more generous state benefits
- increases in the national minimum wage
- changes in the taxation system, e.g. taxing luxury goods heavily
- promoting economic growth
- encouraging of startups and promoting business growth
- job creation
- the provision of free services, such as education and healthcare, and investment to improve them
- investment in training to give people more skills (although these take time to take effect)
- subsidies for certain services, e.g. subsidies for childcare to enable more people to take a job.

Quick test

1. Define 'absolute poverty'.
2. Define 'relative poverty'.
3. Give **two** possible causes of poverty.
4. Give **two** effects of poverty.
5. State **two** possible ways of reducing poverty.

Population

The factors that affect population growth

Population measures the total number of people in a country at a given moment. It is affected by:

- **birth rate** – usually measured by the number of live births per thousand people in the population per year
- **death rate** – usually measured by the number of deaths per thousand people in the population per year
- **fertility rate** – the average number of children a woman will give birth to over her lifetime
- **net migration** – the difference between the number of people entering a country and the number leaving over a period:
  - **net immigration** occurs when the number entering a country exceeds the number leaving over that period
  - **net emigration** occurs when the number leaving a country exceeds the number entering over that period.

The number of people entering and leaving a country depends on the:

- perceived quality of life in different countries
- standard of living in different countries
- ease of entering and leaving different countries, e.g. visa controls
- ease of travel.

The birth and death rates in a country depends on many factors:

The health of the population
- Better healthcare and diet can reduce infant mortality and lead to longer life expectancy.

Education
- Better education can ensure that people know how to reduce infection and disease, how to eat properly and the importance of a healthy lifestyle.
- If there are more women educated, entering and staying in the workforce, it may reduce the birth rate.

Social provisions
- Good social care can mean that older people are better looked after and live longer.
- Clean water can reduce diseases, such as cholera, and reduce the death rate.

Cultural factors
- In some cultures, there is social pressure to have large families, which increases birth rates.
- In some religions, birth control is opposed, which increases the birth rate.

You must be able to:
- describe the factors that affect population growth
- discuss reasons for different rates of population growth in different countries
- describe the effects of an ageing population on an economy.

Political factors

- Government policies will determine the benefits available to those with children in relation to the rewards from working, which will affect the birth rate.
- Some countries have policies that encourage smaller families.
- Government policies will determine the benefits available to the elderly, which will impact on their standard of living and may affect life expectancy.

Environmental factors

- Some countries are vulnerable to natural disasters and disease, due to the climate, and / or have high levels of pollution – these may affect the birth and death rates.

The effects of changes in the size and structure of the population

The **population structure** examines how the population is divided up between males and females of different age groups. It is often shown on a population pyramid.

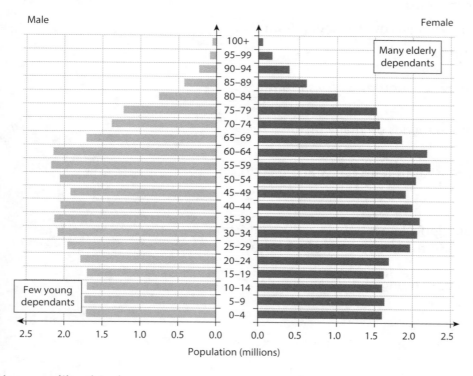

Diagrams like this show:

- how many people there are within working age
- how many young and elderly people there are who may be dependent on those in work for support.

An **ageing population** occurs if the median age of the population increases. This could be due to:

- lower birth rates
- declining fertility rates
- lower death rates, e.g. due to better healthcare.

With an ageing population:

- more people may become dependent on those in work, which may lead to higher taxes for those in work
- there may be a shortage of labour, as there may be fewer people available for work.

The **optimum population** is a theoretical number. It is the population size at which, working with all available resources, there would be the highest standard of living for all people in the country. The optimum population figure can change. With improvements in technology and new resources, the optimum population may increase.

Underpopulation occurs when there are too few people in an area to use the resources effectively, given the level of technology. An increase in the population would lead to a more effective use of resources and an increased standard of living for all people. Underpopulated areas tend to have high average incomes and low unemployment, which may attract people into the area.

Overpopulation occurs when there are too many people in a country given the resources available – if the population reduced, living standards would increase.

Population growth refers to the increase or decrease in the size of the population:

- The population will decline if death rate is greater than birth rate.
- The population will increase if death rate is less than birth rate.

Within an economy, the **dependency ratio** measures the percentage of dependants (under or above working age) compared to the number of people of working age (economically active).

Quick test

1. What is meant by 'an ageing population'?
2. Define 'net migration'.
3. State **one** influence on the death rate.
4. State **one** factor that may lead to more immigration.
5. Give **one** consequence of an ageing population.

Differences in economic development between countries

Classification of economies

As of July 2017, the World Bank income classifications by GNI per capita (US$) are as follows:

- Low-income: < $1005
- Lower-middle income: $1006 to $3955
- Upper-middle income: $3956 to $12 235
- High-income: > $12 235

Low and middle income economies are sometimes referred to as developing economies.

Features of developing and more developed economies

Although each developing country is different, they often display the same characteristics:

- relatively low income per person
- low level of productivity
- high levels of natural resources
- very dependent on primary product exports
- high levels of external debt
- large numbers of people living in agricultural areas
- fast population growth
- relatively young population
- poor infrastructure (e.g. telecommunications, transport and energy)
- political and economic instability
- corruption within the system.

By comparison, a developed economy typically:

- has a relatively high income per person
- is usually industrialised
- has higher literacy rates
- has good infrastructure
- has high life expectancy
- has low birth rates
- has high death rates
- has good housing
- has safe water supplies
- has good access to medical care.

> You must be able to:
> - explain the difference between a developing and developed economy.

The importance of trade in developing economies

Trade can be an important part of the development of an economy because it can provide:

- an increase in aggregate demand through exports
- more jobs, leading to more income and demand within the economy
- a source of foreign exchange
- a source of finance to invest in technology and innovation.

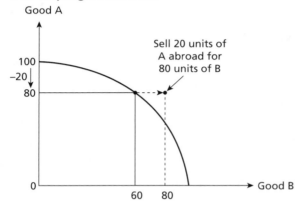

However, trade can cause problems for developing economies, e.g. the volatility of some global commodities means that price changes can have major effects on the exporting economy.

Quick test

1. What is a 'developing economy'?
2. In a developing economy, income per person tends to be low. True or false?
3. In a developing economy, the population tends to be relatively young. True or false?
4. Developing economies are often dependent on primary products. True or false?
5. Describe **one** way in which developed economies may help developing economies.

Exam-style practice questions

1 Which will increase the level of economic development in a country? [1]

  a) a higher infant mortality rate

  b) a higher inflation rate

  c) a higher interest rate

  d) a higher literacy rate

2 Which is **most** likely to reduce the average age of the population in a developed country? [1]

  a) a fall in the birth rate

  b) a fall in the death rate

  c) an increase in emigration

  d) an increase in immigration

3 Which is **most** likely to be found in a typical developing country? [1]

  a) a good education sector

  b) a small average family size

  c) a small percentage of very old people

  d) high spending on entertainment

4 The standard of living in a country is usually measured by [1]

  a) consumer price index.

  b) real national income.

  c) real national income per capita.

  d) real price per capita.

5 The Human Development Index is made up of measures of [1]

  a) health, education and standard of living.

  b) health, education and wealth.

  c) health, wealth and standard of living.

  d) wealth, education and standard of living.

Fig. 1: National income per person (US$)

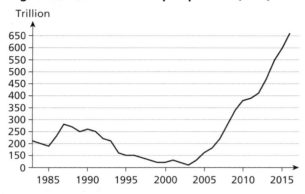

Fig. 2: GDP composition by sector of origin (2016)

Sector of origin	% of GDP
agriculture	36.2
industry	17.0
services	46.8

The Ethiopian economy is growing fast. After years of famine and low growth, the country has experienced high levels of foreign investment more recently, much of which has come from China. The result has been an economic boom. However, average incomes remain very low – the per capita income of $590 is substantially lower than the regional average.

In the last 10 years, Ethiopia has grown on average by more than 10% a year. The country is Africa's second most populous country with a population of over 99 million people and has become the largest economy in East Africa according to the International Monetary Fund.

As costs rise in other countries, Ethiopia is aiming to become a global manufacturing base for foreign companies. The government wants to move the country from an agricultural economy to one where the secondary and tertiary sectors are more dominant.

The country is near seaports, has a large workforce, low wage levels and cheap power. Investment in industry is supported by the government. It is opening industrial areas, where setting up and running businesses will be cheaper and easier, and aims to create 200 000 jobs every year until 2025.

While 55.3% of Ethiopians lived in extreme poverty in 2000, by 2011 this figure was reduced to 33.5% (based on the international poverty line of less than $1.90 per day). Over the past two decades, there has been significant progress in key human development indicators: primary school enrolments are four times higher than they were, child mortality has been cut in half, and the number of people with access to clean water has more than doubled.

However, the challenges facing the government remain significant. For example, the economy needs to grow fast to support the 2.3m Ethiopians that are born every year. It also needs major investment in education: at the moment 80% of young people in the countryside do not finish primary school and 75% of the population still rely on subsistence farming for their livelihood.

a) What is meant by 'a developing economy'? [2]

b) What is meant by 'the tertiary sector'? [2]

c) What is meant by 'the per capita income'? [2]

d) Explain the challenges that still face Ethiopia. [4]

e) Explain why the Ethiopian government has a target of economic growth. [4]

f) Explain why foreign companies may want to invest in Ethiopia. [4]

g) Discuss whether the development of Ethiopia is best measured by the income per person. [6]

h) Discuss how greater trade may help an economy such as Ethiopia. [6]

7 China has experienced fast economic growth helped partly by allowing investment of multinationals into the economy. However, China remains a developing country and has high levels of poverty. According to China's current poverty standard (per capita rural net income of RMB 2300 per year), there were 55 million poor in rural areas in 2015. China also faces demographic pressures related to an ageing population. The extent of poverty, both absolute and relative, is a major problem in many countries.

a) Define 'fast economic growth'. [2]

b) Explain the possible causes of poverty in a country. [4]

c) Analyse the possible consequences of an ageing population. [6]

d) Discuss whether encouraging multinational companies to locate to a country is likely to significantly reduce the extent of poverty there. [8]

8 India's human development index (HDI) value of 0.624 puts it in the 'medium human development' category, alongside countries such as Congo, Namibia and Pakistan. Absolute and relative poverty are significant issues in India, despite having one of the fastest-growing economies in the world, with national income growing at 7.6% in 2011. According to the World Bank in 2016, India had 17.5% of the total world population but a 20.6% share of the world's poorest. In 2011 India's poverty rate for the period 2011–12 stood at 12.4% of the total population, or about 172 million people; taking the poverty line as $1.90 a day. The country has a high birth rate, which affects its population structure.

a) Define 'absolute poverty'. [2]

b) Explain how a high birth rate can affect the population structure. [4]

c) Analyse how changes in gross domestic product (GDP) per head may differ from changes in the Human Development Index. [6]

d) Discuss whether increasing the minimum wage is the best way to reduce poverty in a country. [8]

International specialisation

Specialisation at a national level

International trade occurs when one country sells and buys goods and services from another. It involves **exports** (sales abroad) and **imports** (purchases from abroad).

Trade occurs because one country can produce products at a lower opportunity cost than another.

Specialisation occurs when a country or region specialises in producing the product where it has a comparative advantage.

Advantages and disadvantages of specialisation

A country or region can benefit from trade and specialisation by:

* growing faster than it could on its own
* enjoying a wider range of goods and services at lower prices than it could produce on its own.

The benefits of trade may be even greater than those suggested if there are gains from specialising, e.g. if by doubling resources in an industry, output more than doubles (this is called **increasing returns**).

Specialisation can also lead to economies of scale because of the greater scale of production. This reduces the unit cost and can make the country or region even more price competitive when trading.

Production Possibility Curve (PPC)

A country can sell some of the output of the product where it has comparative advantage abroad (e.g. product X) for more of other products (e.g. product Y) than it could produce domestically. This means it can now consume outside the PPC.

For example:

- Country A produces only 100 units of X.
- It exports 30 of these units to Country B, which is inefficient at producing X itself but efficient at producing Y.
- Country A is able to sell the 30 units of X for 60 units of Y (this is still cheaper for Country B than trying to produce X itself).
- 60 units is a greater number of Y than Country A would have produced had it transferred resources out of Industry X and into Industry Y domestically.

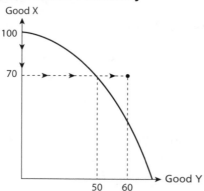

Production Possibility

Quick test

1. Define 'comparative advantage'.
2. A country should specialise in the production of goods and services where it has a comparative advantage. True or false?
3. Give **one** reason why a country may have a comparative advantage in the production of a product.
4. Suggest **one** advantage of specialisation for consumers.
5. State **one** benefit of specialisation for an economy.

Free trade and protection

Globalisation and multinational companies (MNCs)

Globalisation is the process by which the links between countries increase. This is because of developments in communication and transport and greater trade between countries.

A **multinational company (MNC)** is a company that has production bases in more than one country. A business may want to become a multinational to:

- benefit from resources overseas, e.g. cheaper labour, cheaper land, access to resources such as minerals and oil
- gain access to new markets, e.g. by being based within a country, a company may overcome some trade barriers that prevent companies outside the country from selling to it
- gain rewards from the local government, e.g. some governments will offer incentives (such as lower taxes or subsidies) to multinationals to set up base in their country
- reduce risk, e.g. by having bases in more than one country a company has less risk if there is political damage, an environmental disaster or a strike by employees in one country.

The benefits of MNCs

To the host country
MNCs can:
- bring jobs and increase incomes – this has a direct effect on the employees of the MNC, who then spend their money on local goods and services, which increases demand and incomes there; this money will then be spent on other goods and services, and so on
- bring technology and expertise – other businesses will learn from this and gain as well.

To the home country
MNCs can:
- earn profits, which can be returned to the home country and lead to more investment there
- benefit from lower costs and more resources than at home, which leads to more profits for the company's owners.

> **You must be able to:**
> - define 'globalisation'
> - explain the role of multinational companies
> - explain the benefits and costs of multinational companies
> - understand the meaning and benefits of free trade
> - understand the meaning of and reasons for protectionism.

The costs of MNCs

To the host country

An MNC may:

- exploit the country's resources and not invest the profits locally
- abuse its power, e.g. pushing down wages, demanding less regulation or subsidies
- not train local staff, e.g. it may use cheaper local labour for low skill jobs only
- use up resources and relocate once they have gone
- force local businesses to close
- replace national culture with global brands / culture, e.g. change culture of country to become less distinctive nationally and more global.

To home country

An MNC may:

- take jobs abroad
- invest in technology and training abroad rather than at home.

Free trade

Free trade occurs when there are no barriers to trade, current account of balance of payments, i.e. countries can trade with each other without any restrictions.

Barriers to trade include:

- **quotas** – limits on the number of foreign goods and services that can be sold in a country
- **tariffs** – taxes on foreign goods and services
- regulations that make it more difficult or expensive to sell into the country
- legislation that protects certain industries, e.g. laws that insist that services in some industries are provided by domestic firms only
- **export subsidies** – if a government provides aid to domestic producers, it will shift the domestic supply downwards by the subsidy because costs have been reduced
- **embargoes** – when a country bans trade in particular goods and services with another country, often for political reasons.

The benefits of free trade are:

- a country can specialise in the production of goods and services where it has a comparative advantage and export these items at a profit
- a country can buy in goods and services where it does not have a comparative advantage at a price that is lower than it could produce them for itself
- a country's consumers will have a wider choice of goods and services from around the world
- a country can consume outside of its production possibility curve (PPC).

Protection

Protectionism occurs when there are barriers to trade. **Protectionist measures** are designed to protect one country's producers from competition abroad.

Protectionism may occur when governments want to:

- protect 'infant industries' – these are startup businesses that need protecting against more established overseas businesses (that have economies of scale and can sell at such a low price that domestic firms could not compete); protecting the infant industries allows them to grow, gain internal economies of scale and eventually be able to compete internationally
- protect key strategic industries, such as defence and agriculture, to ensure the country is not overly reliant on foreign firms in case of war (this is a political reason not an economic one)
- protect / support an industry that is struggling, perhaps because it has lost its comparative advantage and international competitiveness
- retaliate against the protectionist actions of other governments
- protect against dumping, i.e. when a country sells some products at a loss to destroy the foreign competition.

Protectionism can lead to:

- less choice for a country's consumers
- higher prices for a country's consumers, which can lead to inflation
- less competition for domestic producers, which may reduce quality and customer service
- more protection for domestic producers, which may allow inefficient producers to survive and increase the profits of certain domestic industries
- fewer exports for other countries, which may reduce income and growth in these countries.

Revision tip

Some of the arguments for protectionism are political reasons rather than economic reasons.

Quick test

1. What is the term for a tax placed on foreign goods and services?
2. What is the term for a limit placed on the number of goods allowed into a country?
3. What is the name given to startup industries that may need protection to enable them to become more internationally competitive?
4. Explain what is meant by 'retaliation' in relation to protectionism.
5. Give **one** argument against protectionism.

Foreign exchange rates

Foreign exchange rates

An **exchange rate** is the price of one currency in terms of another, e.g. the number of euros received in exchange for one dollar. There are many exchanges rates, such as the value of the dollar in euros, pounds, yen and yuan.

In a **floating exchange rate** system, the price of a currency is determined by market forces, i.e. by the supply and demand of the currency in the foreign currency markets:

*   If the price of the currency increases, the currency is getting 'stronger' – this is an **appreciation** of the currency.
*   If the price of the currency decreases, the currency is getting 'weaker' – this is a **depreciation** of the currency.

Determination of the foreign exchange rate

Demand for a currency

Demand for a currency is the demand from others to convert their currency into this one. It shows the quantity demanded at each and every exchange rate, all other factors unchanged. A change in the exchange rate leads to a movement along the demand curve.

This demand for a currency depends on factors such as:

*   the demand for the country's goods and services
*   the attractiveness of saving in the country– the higher the domestic interest rate, the more likely it is that people or firms will want to invest in the country
*   speculation:
    *   if speculators believe a currency is going to fall in value in the future, they will sell now – this reduces demand
    *   if speculators believe that a currency will increase in value in the future, they will buy now – this increases demand
*   the behavior of MNCs:
    *   if MNCs want to invest in a country, it will increase demand for the currency – this type of investment is called foreign direct investment (FDI)
    *   if MNCs are leaving a country, they will need less currency, so demand for the currency falls.

A change in any of these factors (other than exchange rate) leads to a shift in the demand curve.

The demand for the currency is downward sloping. As the exchange rate increases in value, it makes exports more expensive in foreign currency. The higher the price in foreign currency, the lower the sales and, therefore, the lower the amount of domestic currency earned.

The slope of the demand for the currency will depend on the price elasticity of demand for exports. The more price elastic demand for exports is:

*   the greater the fall in sales given an increase in the exchange rate
*   the greater the fall in domestic currency.

> **You must be able to:**
> *   understand what is meant by an 'exchange rate'
> *   understand the meaning of a 'floating exchange rate'
> *   understand what determines equilibrium in the exchange rate market
> *   explain the reasons why an exchange rate may increase or decrease in value
> *   explain the consequences of exchange rate fluctuations.

> **Revision tip**
>
> The exchange rate is the external value of the currency – it is its price in terms of other currencies.

Example

Price of US product = $100
Sales of product = 500 units
Export earnings = 500 × $100 = $50 000

The exchange rate increases by 10%.
Assume sales fall by 20% (this means the price elasticity of demand for exports is –2).
Sales would now be 400 and export earnings would be 400 × £100 = $40 000

If sales only fell by 1% (in which case the price elasticity of demand is –0.1), they would be 495 units. Export earnings would now be 495 × $100 = $49 500

The more price elastic the demand for exports:

- the more an increase in the value of the exchange rate will reduce export earnings
- the more price elastic the demand for the currency is.

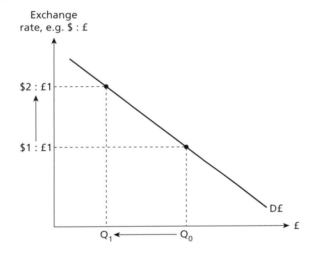

Supply of a currency

The **supply** of a currency shows the quantity supplied of a currency to the foreign exchange market at each and every exchange rate, all other factors unchanged. A change in the exchange rate leads to a movement along the supply curve.

The supply of a currency to the foreign currency market depends on the desire to change this currency into another currency. This depends on factors such as:

- the demand for foreign goods and services
- the interest rate abroad (how attractive saving in a foreign currency would be)
- speculation, e.g. if speculators believe a currency will fall, they may sell it now – this increases the quantity supplied.

A change in any of these factors (other than exchange rate) leads to a shift in the supply curve – more or less currency is supplied at each and every exchange rate.

The shape of the supply curve for a currency depends on the price elasticity of demand for imports. An increase in the exchange rate reduces the local price of imports. If the demand for imports is price elastic, the increase is the quantity demanded is relatively high and the total spending on imports increases. With the higher exchange rate, the spending on imports increases and the supply of the currency increases. The supply of the currency is upward sloping.

If the demand for imports is price inelastic, the increase in the quantity demanded is relatively low and the total spending on imports decreases. With the higher exchange rate, the spending on imports decreases and the supply of the currency decreases. The supply of the currency is downward sloping.

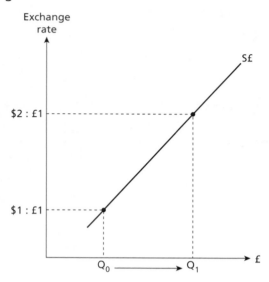

Equilibrium in the foreign currency market

Assuming a downward-sloping demand curve for the currency and an upward-sloping supply curve for the currency:

- If the exchange rate is below equilibrium, there is excess demand for the currency. The value will increase, which reduces quantity demanded and increases the quantity supplied until equilibrium is reached.
- If the exchange rate is above equilibrium, there is excess supply for the currency. The value will decrease, which increases the quantity demanded and decreases the quantity supplied until equilibrium is reached.

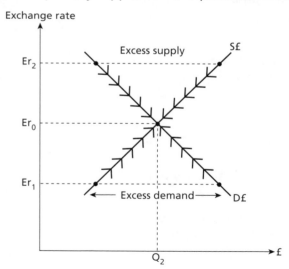

The effect of changes in supply and demand for a currency

Change in supply and demand conditions	Effect in the market
increase in demand for the currency	increases the exchange rate and quantity
decrease in demand for the currency	decreases the exchange rate and quantity
increase in supply of the currency	decreases the exchange rate and increases the quantity
decrease in supply of the currency	increases the exchange rate and reduces the quantity

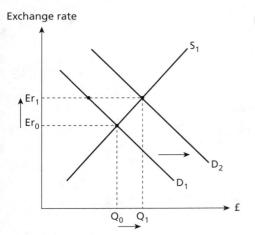

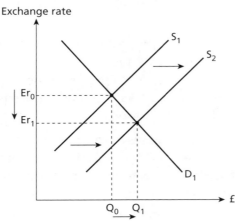

> **Revision tip**
>
> The impact of a change in the exchange rate depends on whether the business is an importer or exporter.

Causes and consequences of fluctuations

Government and exchange rates

A government may make it a policy to keep the exchange rate at a particular level. This is known as a **fixed (or managed) exchange rate** system. The government may want to do this:

- to keep it stable – to help businesses plan and to encourage investment
- to keep it relatively low – to encourage exports (all other things unchanged, a low exchange rate makes exports cheaper in a foreign currency)
- to keep it high – to reduce demand for exports and reduce import prices to dampen inflationary pressures.

Government intervention in currency markets

A government can intervene in the currency market by:

- buying and selling currency:
    - to keep the currency higher in value, the government buys its currency (increasing demand), using up its foreign currency reserves
    - to reduce the value of its currency, the government sells its currency, building up its foreign currency reserves
- changing interest rates:
    - an increase in interest rates attracts demand for the currency from abroad (as more foreign investors want to save that country) and, all other things unchanged, increases its value
    - a decrease in interest rates is likely to reduce demand for the currency and reduce its value.

> **Revision tip**
>
> When explaining the effect of a change in the exchange rate, it is often useful to give a numerical example, e.g. if the US exchange rate falls from $1 : 1€ to $1 : 0.8€, then a $100 product that would have sold at 100€ will now sell at 80€.

The effect of an appreciation of the currency

A stronger currency (due to an appreciation) will make a country's goods and services more expensive in the foreign currency, all other factors unchanged. For example, if a product is $5 and the exchange rate is $1 : 10 yen, then this product will sell for 50 yen abroad. If the exchange rate increases to $1 : 20 yen, then the same product will now sell for 100 yen. This will reduce the quantity demanded of exports and the earnings in the domestic currency.

The greater the price elasticity of demand for exports, the greater the fall in export earnings.

A strong currency will also make imports cheaper in the domestic currency. For example, if a product is 60 yen and the exchange rate is $1 : 10 yen, then this product will cost $6. If the exchange rate increases to $1 : 20 yen, then the same product will now cost $3. This will reduce costs and can, over time, improve the profits of the business.

The extent to which demand for imports increases in response to a fall in price depends on the price elasticity of demand for imports. The greater the price elasticity, the more sensitive demand is to price changes. This means that an appreciation of currency may mean:

- fewer export sales for firms
- cheaper foreign components for firms
- cheaper imported product for consumers.

A depreciation of the currency

A depreciation of a currency means it loses value – it becomes cheaper in terms of other currencies. This may be because of less demand or more supply.

A depreciation means:

- exports are cheaper in foreign currencies, which should increase sales and export revenue – the scale of the impact depends on the price elasticity of demand for exports
- imports are more expensive in domestic currency and:
  - the total spending on imports will fall if demand for imports is price elastic
  - the total spending on imports increases if the demand for imports is price inelastic.

Quick test

1. What is meant by an 'exchange rate'?
2. Explain why an exchange rate may increase in value.
3. What is the term given to an increase in the value of a currency?
4. Give **one** reason why a currency may fall in value.
5. Explain how an increase in the exchange rate may affect the costs of imports.

The structure of the current account of balance of payments

The **balance of payments** is a record of all of a country's financial transactions with the rest of the world over a year. It has three elements:

* the current account
* the capital account
* the financial account.

The current account

The current account is made up of the:

* **balance of trade** (trade in goods and services account)
* **primary income** account
* **secondary income** account.

The balance of these accounts is known as the current account balance.

The balance of trade

The balance of trade measures the difference between the value of:

* **exports**, i.e. goods and services that are made by a country and sold abroad – these represent money coming into the country
* **imports**, i.e. goods and services made abroad and sold to people within the country – these represent money leaving the country.

The balance of trade can be divided even further by analysing the:

* trade in goods (visible trade), e.g. cars, electronics or machinery
* trade in services (invisible trade), e.g. banking, education or management consultancy.

Primary income

Primary income is made up of income earned by a country's citizens who own assets overseas. It includes earnings, profits, dividends on investments abroad (payments made to shareholders by companies who earn a profit) and interest. This is export income.

Import spending is made up of the profits and dividends earned in a country but belonging to foreign citizens.

Secondary income

Secondary income involves:

* money transfers between central governments (who lend and borrow money from each other)
* grants, such as those that a country may receive as part of the Common Agricultural Policy if it is part of the European Union (EU).

The current account position of a country

The current account position of a country on the balance of payments will depend on:

Exchange rates

If the value of a currency increases, it makes exports more expensive overseas in other currencies. This reduces sales and export revenue and worsens the current account position.

> **You must be able to:**
> * describe the structure of the current account of balance of payments
> * explain what is meant by a current account 'deficit' or 'surplus' on the balance of payments
> * understand the possible reasons for a current account deficit or surplus
> * explain policies to achieve stability on the balance of payments.

The extent of the effect on export revenue depends on how much the value of currency changes and the price elasticity of demand for exports.

A stronger currency will also make imports cheaper in the domestic currency, which is likely to lead to less spending on imports.

Relative inflation rates

Relative inflation rates will affect the relative prices of a country's goods abroad and, therefore, how competitive its goods and services are. For example, relatively high inflation rates tend to make a country's products uncompetitive abroad, all other things unchanged, and will reduce export revenue.

Income level

The income level of a country will affect its spending on imports. The income of other countries will affect how much they are likely to buy. This will affect its exports and may lead to more imports.

Productivity

Increasing productivity in a country will reduce the unit costs of production, all other factors unchanged. This is likely to make a country's goods and services more attractive abroad.

Current account balance calculations

	Year 1 ($bn)	Year 2 ($bn)
export earnings from goods and services	200	200
import spending on goods and services	160	220
balance of trade (export earnings – import spending)	40	–20
primary income balance (inflows – outflows)	10	5
secondary income balance (inflows – outflows)	–5	2
current account balance (balance of trade + primary income balance + secondary income balance)	45 (surplus)	–13 (deficit)

Current account deficit and surplus

If there is a current account **deficit**, then the value of money leaving the country on the current account is greater than the value of money entering the country.

If there is a current account **surplus**, then the value of money entering the country on the current account is greater than the value of money leaving the country.

A current account deficit may mean:

- a country is importing a higher volume of goods and services than it is exporting – this may improve living standards, because consumers are consuming more products
- a country is importing valuable capital equipment – this will improve its productive capacity in the long run.

Therefore, in the short run, a current account deficit may not be a problem. However, having higher import spending than export earnings reduces aggregate demand, which can lead to unemployment.

In the long run, a current account deficit can:

- reduce jobs in domestic industries
- reflect a long-term underlying lack of competitiveness
- lead to a fall in the value of the currency and high import prices, which causes cost-push inflation.

Policies to achieve stability

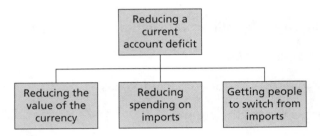

Reducing the value of the currency

Reducing the value of the currency reduces the price of exports, all other factors unchanged, and makes the price of imports higher in the domestic currency. It should increase earnings from exports and usually reduces spending on imports. This should reduce the deficit. However, the higher import prices may, over time, cause cost-push inflation.

Reducing spending on imports by reducing income

The government may use policies aimed at reducing total spending in an economy (increased taxes, reduced public spending or raised interest rates). This will reduce aggregate demand, which reduces spending on imports. However, the effect is to reduce spending generally, which can lead to slower growth and unemployment.

Policies aimed at getting people to switch away from imports

Policies can be aimed at getting consumers to switch away from foreign products to domestic products. They include tariffs (taxes on foreign products) and quotas (limits on the number of imported items). However, these measures lead to higher prices for consumers and less choice. They also allow inefficient domestic producers to produce because they are protected.

Quick test

1. Define 'the current account on the balance of payments'.
2. What is meant by a current account 'deficit'?
3. Explain why a country may have a current account deficit on its balance of payments.
4. Explain how a current account deficit may affect inflation.
5. Explain how a government may use the exchange rate to reduce a deficit on the current account.

Exam-style practice questions

1 Which change is **most** likely to increase the demand for imports? [1]

a) an increase in income tax rates

b) an increase in tariffs imposed by the government

c) an increase in the cost of consumer borrowing

d) an increase in the exchange rate

2 Which is likely to lead to an increase in the size of a country's current account deficit? [1]

a) an increase in the competitiveness of domestic goods

b) an increase in the earnings of foreign investors in domestic companies

c) an increase in the number of overseas visitors to the country

d) an increase in quotas

3 Which could **not** be a reason for imposing tariffs on imported goods? [1]

a) to encourage self-sufficient production within an economy

b) to lower the general price level within the economy

c) to protect a new and growing domestic industry

d) to reduce the current account deficit on the balance of payments

4 Which action will the government take in a fixed exchange rate system? [1]

a) It will buy its currency if there is a shortage in the foreign exchange market.

b) It will buy its currency if there is excess demand in the foreign exchange market.

c) It will sell its currency if there is excess demand in the foreign exchange market.

d) It will sell its currency if there is excess supply in the foreign exchange market.

5 **Trade between JAPAN and the EU**

In 2017, the European Union (EU) and Japan, two of the world's biggest economic areas, agreed a deal that would allow free trade between them.

Japan is the EU's second biggest trading partner in Asia after China. It is also the seventh biggest export market for European producers. Imports from Japan to the EU are mainly machinery, electrical equipment, motor vehicles, optical and medical instruments, and chemicals. EU exports to Japan are mainly motor vehicles, machinery, pharmaceuticals, optical and medical instruments, and electrical equipment.

One of the most important trade categories for the EU is dairy goods. The EU's dairy farmers have been struggling due to falling prices within Europe. Farmers say they are paid less than the cost of production. They sell their milk mainly to the large supermarkets. However, demand for milk and milk-based products in Japan has been growing steadily in recent years.

Exporters from the EU pay €1 billion ($1.1 billion) in export duties to Japan each year, with tariffs of around 20% on agricultural products. The trade deal will reduce Japanese tariffs on beef, pork, wine, textiles, clothing and shoes. Meanwhile tariffs on Japanese cars sold in the EU will be lowered from their present 10% over seven years.

Some commentators think the deal may increase the value of the EU's exports to Japan by 34%, and Japan's to the EU by 29%. Because of the potential impact on domestic industries, the deal is likely to have long transition clauses of up to 15 years to allow sectors in both countries to adjust.

Fig. 1: Japan's income and population, 2016

Income	$4.932 trillion
Population	127 million

Fig. 2: EU–Japan trade and investment

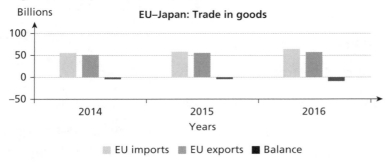

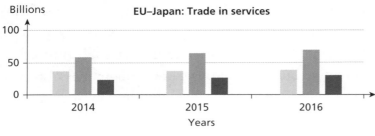

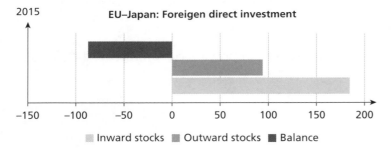

a) State whether the EU balance of trade in goods between the EU and Japan was in surplus or deficit in 2016. **[1]**

b) Describe what is meant by the 'European Union'. **[2]**

c) Define 'free trade'. **[2]**

d) Explain the possible reasons why Japan is the EU's second biggest trading partner. **[4]**

e) Explain why the EU–Japan trade deal is likely to have a 15-year transition period for businesses to adjust. **[4]**

f) Calculate the average income per person in Japan in 2016. [2]

g) Explain why the EU may export motor vehicles to Japan *and* import motor vehicles from Japan. [4]

h) Explain why the price of milk might have been falling in the EU. [5]

i) With reference to Fig. 2, discuss whether the EU–Japan trade deal is a good idea. [6]

6 The world's top 60 economies have adopted more than 7000 protectionist trade measures since the financial crisis in 2008. Tariffs are now worth more than $400 billion. These are used to raise revenue and to try and aid current account deficit. The United States and European Union were each responsible for more than 1000 of the restrictions. The impact of protectionism and any retaliation depends on how much trade a country undertakes. In the United States, for example, trade as a percentage of its GDP is around 28 per cent. Russia and Germany have much higher trade to GDP ratios of 51 per cent and 86 per cent respectively.

a) Define 'current account deficit of the balance of payments'. [2]

b) Explain two methods of trade protection that a country could use. [4]

c) Analyse the reasons why a government might introduce protectionism. [6]

d) Discuss whether trade protection is always preferable to free trade. [8]

7 Turkey's current account deficit reached $5.1 billion in July 2017, bringing the annual deficit to $37.1 billion in total. The increase in the current account deficit was mainly due to the rise in the deficit in goods items by nearly $3.8 billion to $7.3 billion in the month. Travel items, which constitute a major part of the services account, recorded a net inflow of $2.3 billion in July. Secondary income recorded a net inflow of $226 million. The overall deficit is expected to lead to a fall in Turkey's exchange rate, which may improve the current account position. The government may also introduce protectionism.

a) Define 'exchange rate'. [2]

b) Explain why a country might have a deficit in its goods trade. [4]

c) Analyse the possible effect of protectionism on different economic agents. [6]

d) Discuss whether a fall in the exchange rate is likely to improve a current account deficit. [8]

Answers

Marking your answer

For each exam-style practice question in this book, to help you mark your own answers, the key points that should be included in an effective answer are listed. However, it is important to remember that answers should be communicated in a clear, accurate and well-developed way. The questions, example answers, marks awarded and comments that appear in this book were written by the author. In examinations, the way marks would be awarded to answers like these may be different.

1 The basic economic problem

The nature of the economic problem
1. The production of an economic good has an opportunity cost; a free good does not
2. Resources that are limited and can be used up
3. Any three from: consumers / households; employees / workers; producers / firms / businesses; governments
4. Given the limited resources and unlimited wants, an economy must decide what to produce, how to produce, and who to produce it for
5. A resource that can be replaced / comes from a sustainable source, e.g. trees

Factors of production
1. A willingness and ability to take risks to develop business ideas
2. Any three from: land; labour; capital; enterprise
3. By investment (in machinery and equipment)
4. There are barriers / factors that prevent people moving between jobs and locations
5. Through training
6. Someone who identifies business opportunities and is willing to take the risk to invest in them

Opportunity cost and the production possibility curve diagram (PPC)
1. It is what is given up / sacrificed in the next best alternative when a decision is made
1. The maximum goods and services that can be produced in an economy at a given time
2. As resources are transferred from one industry to another, output of one product (e.g. B) increases and output of the other product (e.g. A) falls; the amount of A given up to produce the extra amount of B is the opportunity cost
3. No more of one product can be produced without reducing production of another
4. With more or better resources, the maximum goods and services that can be produced can increase

Exam-style practice questions
1. C **[1 mark]**
2. A **[1 mark]**
3. D **[1 mark]**
4. D **[1 mark]**
5. B **[1 mark]**
6. A **[1 mark]**
7. a) 2015 population = 52 million
   1960 population = 25 million
   Percentage change = [(52 − 25) ÷ 25] × 100 **[1]** = 108% **[1]**
   [2 marks]
   b) It involves the extractive industries **[1]**, i.e. the first stage of production such as farming and oil **[1]**. **[2 marks]**
   c) It means the national income of the country **[1]** is growing at a rapid rate **[1]**. **[2 marks]**

d) The PPC curve will shift outwards **[1]**; if there is an increase in the quantity or quality of a country's resources **[1]**. Your answer must include a clear and accurately labelled diagram of the PPC shifting outwards **[1]** showing growth **[1]**. **[4 marks]**
e) Explanations which might include:
   - an investment in capital may lead to an increase in the quantity of capital **[1]** and / or the quality of capital **[1]**; this can improve the productivity of the other resources in the economy **[1]**, which would increase the capacity of the economy **[1]**. **[4 marks]**
f) Coherent analysis which might include:
   - a country can specialise in producing what it is good at **[1]** and sell it abroad in return for more of other goods **[1]** than it could produce itself **[1]**; if each country specialises in what it is good at it can lead to more consumption **[1]**. **[4 marks]**
g) Award up to 4 marks for logical reasons why investment in education can lead to an improvement in skills, e.g. explain how an improvement in skills can lead to greater productivity and, therefore, economic growth.
   Award up to 4 marks for logical reasons why investment in education may not lead to an improvement in skills, e.g. depends on what money is spent on and how it is used, e.g. are people trained in the correct skills. **[6 marks]**
h) Your answer should:
   Award up to 4 marks for logical reasons why producing capital goods may be better because it will lead to more output in the future but involve a sacrifice of resources, i.e. if an economy puts resources into capital goods, the opportunity cost is less consumption now.
   Award up to 4 marks for logical reasons why producing consumption goods may be better because it will mean more is consumed now but there is less investment for the future. **[6 marks]**
8. a) Every decision involves a commitment of resources that could have been used elsewhere; therefore, there is always a sacrifice, i.e. an opportunity cost for every decision **[1]**. More spending on education means less spending on something else given the budget available **[1]**. **[2 marks]**
   b) Explanations which might include:
   - explain how the transfer of resources from one sector to another increases output in the one industry **[1]** but involves a sacrifice of output from the other industry, i.e. there is an opportunity cost **[1]**
   - include an accurately drawn and labelled PPC diagram **[1]** showing less output of one product for more of another **[1]**. **[4 marks]**
   c) Coherent analysis which might include:
   - labour is a factor of production **[1]** that affects output **[1]**
   - education affects skills and productivity **[1]**; it improves the quality of labour **[1]**
   - low investment means that workers are likely to produce less **[1]**; this reduces output and is likely to reduce economic growth, all other factors constant **[1]**. **[6 marks]**

d) **Explain why opportunity costs are important to consumers,** e.g. when deciding how best to spend their income. Any decision involves an opportunity cost. You could give an example, e.g. if they have to buy school clothes for their child, they may not have enough money to buy other goods.

   Explain why opportunity costs are important to other economic agents, for example:
   - the government, when deciding whether to invest in a particular area of the economy, e.g. education
   - producers / firms, when deciding whether to invest in a project, e.g. what else could they have done with the funds. **[8 marks]**

9. a) Factors of production are used in the production of goods and services **[1]**; they are land, labour, capital and enterprise **[1]**. **[2 marks]**

   b) Explanations which might include:
   - the scarcity of resources at any time **[1]** and the unlimited wants **[1]**
   - the need to allocate resources and make choices **[1]** about what to produce, how to produce it, and who to produce it for **[1]**. **[4 marks]**

   c) Coherent analysis which might include:
   - an improvement in the quality **[1]**, e.g. more training **[1]** or better management **[1]**
   - increase in the quantity of factors of production **[1]**, e.g. more labour due to birth rates **[1]** or immigration **[1]**, more capital **[1]**, more land (e.g. reclamation) **[1]**, better technology **[1]**. **[6 marks]**

   d) **Explain the benefits of the free market** compared to government intervention, e.g. an incentive to innovate and be efficient to achieve higher profits.

   Explain the problems of the free market and therefore the potential advantages of the command economy, e.g. problems in free market of inequality, price fluctuations, some products being over or under provided. **[8 marks]**

2 The allocation of resources

Micro and macroeconomics
1. A study of what happens in individual markets
2. A study of what happens in the economy as a whole
3. True
4. False
5. False

The role of markets in allocating resources
1. The quantity producers are willing and able to supply at each and every price, all other factors unchanged
2. The quantity consumers are willing and able to buy at each and every price, all other factors unchanged
3. At the given price, the quantity demanded equals the quantity supplied
4. The price adjusts acting as an incentive, a signal and a rationing device to bring about equilibrium in a market
5. Changes in supply and demand conditions

Demand
1. It assumes that all other factors apart from price are held constant / remain unchanged
2. Any one from: the price of a substitute increases; the price of complement falls; there are more people in the buying population; income increases (assuming it is a normal good)
3. Any one from: the price of a substitute decreases; the price of complement increases; there are fewer people in the buying population; income decreases (assuming it is a normal good)

4. A movement along a demand curve is due to a change in price; a shift in demand is due to a change in other factors
5. The market demand curve is the horizontal summation of all the individual demand curves

Supply
1. It assumes that price changes but all other factors are held constant / remain unchanged
2. Any one from: there are more producers; resource prices are lower; technology improves; production subsidies are paid
3. Any one from: there are fewer producers; resource prices are higher; taxes are placed on producers
4. A movement along a supply curve is due to a change in price; a shift in supply occurs due to a change in other factors
5. The market supply curve is the horizontal summation of all the individual supply curves

Price determination
1. The price at which the quantity demanded equals the quantity supplied
2. Surplus
3. Shortage
4. Increase
5. It means the quantity demanded is not equal to the quantity supplied

Price changes
1. a)
2. e)
3. g)
4. c)

Price elasticity of demand (PED)
1. Price elasticity of demand (PED)
   $$= \frac{\% \text{ change in quantity demanded}}{\% \text{ change in price}}$$
2. The percentage change in quantity demanded is less than the percentage change in price
3. Fall
4. Any one from: brand loyalty; improved / increased advertising; ease of switching to another product; the time period being considered
5. Change in sales = −0.5 × 10 = −5%; sales will fall by 5%, i.e. 0.05 × 200 = 10 units; sales will now be (200 − 10 =) 190 units

Price elasticity of supply (PES)
1. Price elasticity of supply (PES) $= \frac{\% \text{ change in quantity supplied}}{\% \text{ change in price}}$
2. The percentage change in quantity supplied is less than the percentage change in price
3. Quantity supplied will increase by 2.5 × 5 = 12.5%
4. Any one from: extent to which there is capacity; ease of increasing production; time period
5. Percentage change in quantity supplied = 0.5 × 2 = 1%. New quantity supplied = 200 + (0.01 × 200) = 202 units

Market economic system
1. Business organisations that are owned by private individuals
2. Business organisations that are owned by the government
3. Government organisations may have social objectives and be less profit focused
4. The economy has a private and a public sector
5. Any one from: the profit motive may lead to efficiency as firms try to cut costs; innovation as firms try to gain more customers; high levels of customer service as firms try to sell more

Market failure

1. A distortion in the market is preventing an efficient allocation of resources
2. The benefit to society is greater than the perceived private benefit; individuals do not fully appreciate the benefits of a good or service
3. The monopoly pushes up the price and reduces output compared to a competitive market; this can be bad for consumers
4. The production of a product may contribute to pollution, congestion or other environmental damage; these are external costs, which means the social cost of production is greater than the private cost (to the firm)
5. Non-diminishable; non-excludable

Mixed economic system

1. It will lead to excess quantity supplied, i.e. a surplus
2. It will lead to an excess quantity demanded, i.e. a shortage
3. It may mean that social costs and benefits are taken into account as the organisation is owned by the government
4. Increases producer costs which, in the case of negative external costs, may increase private costs to become more equal to social costs
5. Indirect tax will increase costs and lead to a higher equilibrium price and lower equilibrium quantity

Exam-style practice questions

1. D   [1 mark]
2. D   [1 mark]
3. B   [1 mark]
4. B   [1 mark]
5. B   [1 mark]
6. D   [1 mark]
7. A   [1 mark]
8. a) If wages stay the same but prices increase, consumer purchasing power will fall [1]; their money will buy less than it could before [1].   [2 marks]
   b) There is a danger [1] that the borrowers will not be able to repay some or all of the amount borrowed [1].
                                                                  [2 marks]
   c) Explanations which might include:
      • there seems to be a strong link between national income growth and house prices [1]
      • this may be because, with more income, demand for houses increases [1], given that supply cannot change quickly [1] it leads to higher prices [1].   [4 marks]
   d) House prices fell significantly [1]; the 'increase' in prices is negative – they are growing at a negative rate [1].
                                                                  [2 marks]
   e) Logical explanation which might include:
      • number of households looking for accommodation [1] and businesses looking for office / factory space; more looking leads to more demand [1]
      • cost and availability of finance [1]; lower cost of borrowing increases demand [1]
      • confidence in the future [1] – households may be reluctant to spend heavily on property if they are worried about the future; businesses may be reluctant to spend on factory / office space if they are worried about the future [1].   [4 marks]
   f) Explanations which might include:
      • use a diagram or diagrams to help explain that prices might be high due to:
         • high demand [1], e.g. due to confidence in the economy [1]
         • limited supply [1], e.g. due to restrictions on building [1].   [4 marks]
   g) Award up to 4 marks for logical reasons why a fall in property prices might impact on one group, for example:
      • impact on consumers – with lower house prices, consumers have fewer assets; with this fall in wealth

they are likely to reduce consumption spending, which will reduce demand in the economy.
Award up to 4 marks for logical reasons why a fall in property prices might impact on another group, e.g.
   • impact on firms – businesses may reduce investment if they regard the lower prices as evidence of less demand in the economy; concerns over lower property prices may lead to less investment and less demand.   [6 marks]
   h) Award up to 4 marks for logical reasons why buying a house might be a good investment because of the potential increase in property prices.
Award up to 4 marks for logical reasons why buying a house might not be a good investment, e.g. explain how there are costs involved and interest payments, so it depends on what happens to the value of the asset relative to these costs; it also depends on whether house prices rise or fall.   [6 marks]
9. a) A shortage shows that the quantity demanded at a given price is greater than the quantity supplied [1] meaning there is excess demand [1].   [2 marks]
   b) Logical explanation which might include:
      • bad weather [1] reducing the amount produced [1]
      • crop disease [1] reducing the output in a given year [1]
      • an increase in number of producers [1] increasing output [1]
      • technology [1] increasing output [1].   [4 marks]
   c) Coherent analysis which might include:
      • accurately labelled supply and demand diagram [1]
      • a supply curve shifting inwards [1]
      • accurately shows the old equilibrium [1] and new equilibrium [1], with a new higher equilibrium price [1] and higher equilibrium quantity [1].   [6 marks]
   d) **Explain when a maximum price has an effect and what that is,** i.e. a maximum price only has an effect if it is below the equilibrium price and maximum price leads to excess demand. Maximum price may be used by the government to make sure that items are affordable, e.g. housing.
Explain the problems of a maximum price, i.e. keeping the price below equilibrium reduces the quantity supplied so less is available than in a free market. It is more affordable for those who get it but fewer consume it.   [8 marks]
10. a) It is a restriction on how low the price can go in a market [1] that aims to keep price below the level it would be at in the free market [1].   [2 marks]
   b) Logical explanation which might include:
      • the nature of the product, e.g. tobacco is addictive [1], and so is likely to be price inelastic demand [1].
      • the availability of substitutes such as e-cigarettes [1]; the more the substitutes the more price elastic demand is [1]
      • the degree of brand loyalty [1]; the more brand loyalty there is the more price inelastic demand is [1]
      • the percentage of income spent on the product [1]; the greater the percentage the more price elastic demand will be [1].   [4 marks]
   c) Coherent analysis which might include:
      • an accurately labelled supply and demand diagram [1]
      • the price fixed above equilibrium [1]
      • quantity supplied with minimum price shown [1] and the quantity demanded [1]; this leads to an excess supply [1]
      • amount of excess supply marked on diagram [1].
                                                                  [6 marks]

d) **Explain the benefits to the government of understanding price elasticity of demand, for example:**
   - understanding price elasticity of demand means the government can anticipate the effect of, e.g. introducing indirect taxes and minimum and maximum prices on the quantity demanded
   - this can help it decide on the level at which these should be set to achieve a desired impact on the quantity demanded.

   Explain that there are factors that limit the value of knowing the price elasticity of demand, for example:
   - the effect in the market of a change in market conditions may also depend on the extent of the shift in demand and supply and the price elasticity of supply
   - the value of the price elasticity of demand will change, e.g. over time the value of the price elasticity of demand may vary. **[8 marks]**

11. a) In a free market resources are allocated by supply and demand [1]. The price mechanism brings supply and demand together [1]. **[2 marks]**
    b) Explanations which might include:
       - that pollution is an external cost [1] which increases the total costs to society [1]
       - that pollution means that in the free market, where only private costs and benefits are considered, there is over-production [1] which is inefficient [1]. **[4 marks]**
    c) Coherent analysis which might include:
       - taxes can be placed on production [1] to increase the private costs [1] to equal the social costs [1]
       - by increasing costs this will shift supply [1] reducing the equilibrium quantity in the market [1]
       - if the tax matches the external cost [1] the level of output will be efficient thanks to this intervention [1]. **[6 marks]**
    d) **Explain the effect of 'tougher standards' on emissions,** e.g. this will force producers to reduce output and this be more efficient than producers ignoring external costs and over-producing.
       Explain the case for taxation, e.g. taxation increases the private costs to force producers to take account of the effects of pollution; taxation raises revenue for the government but raises the price for consumers; this may affect people's ability to travel, especially low income groups. This may be seen as unfair and also affect, e.g. their ability to work. **[8 marks]**

3 Microeconomic decision makers

Money and banking
1. Any three from: unit of account; medium of exchange; standard of deferred payment; store of value
2. Any two from: accept deposits; lend; provide efficient means of payment
3. To manage a country's currency, money supply and interest rates
4. To achieve an inflation target

Households
1. It is the cost of borrowing money and the reward for saving
2. Any two from: income; income tax; consumer confidence
3. Any two from: to save income for later life; to save for a major purchase; to have a safety fund
4. Any one from: different income; different stage of life cycle; time of year
5. An overdraft is a facility to borrow short term up to an agreed limit; a loan is when a fixed sum of money is borrowed for a fixed term at agreed interest rates

Workers
1. Any two from: skills required; nature of job; wages
2. Higher wages
3. Higher wages
4. Limited government funds; often not profit making; may be offset by greater job security or better pensions
5. They may produce more output or higher value output for the business and, therefore, can receive higher rewards

Trade unions
1. An organisation to represent and protect employees
2. Strike
3. Work to rule
4. Redundancies
5. Any one from: help understand an issue from employees' perspective; help gain the cooperation of employees; help find solutions to problems

Firms
1. Any one from: its sales (turnover), what it owns (assets), the number of employees
2. Primary sector: farming / extraction; secondary sector: manufacturing
3. A merger occurs when two or more firms join together to become one new business; a takeover occurs when one firm gains control of another
4. Backward vertical integration occurs when one firm takes over another firm in the same production process but closer to the suppliers; forward vertical integration occurs when one firm takes over another firm in the same production process but closer to the consumers
5. These occur when unit costs fall as the scale of production increases
6. Any one from: to gain economies of scale; to gain market power

Firms and production
1. Land; labour; capital; enterprise
2. Labour productivity = $\dfrac{\text{output}}{\text{number of employees}}$
3. Labour productivity = $\dfrac{400}{80}$ = 5 units
4. Any two from: quantity of capital equipment available; quality of capital equipment available; organisation of work; training received; motivation levels
5. High productivity means that more units can be produced with the same inputs, which should increase sales and revenue, or the same output can be produced with fewer inputs, which should reduce costs

Firms' costs, revenue and objectives
1. Profit = total revenue – total costs
2. Costs that do not change with output
3. Costs that do change with output
4. Average cost = $\dfrac{\text{total cost}}{\text{output}}$ (average cost is total cost per unit)
5. Used to reward owners; used to invest into the business (a source of funds)

Market structure
1. Any two from: better service; better quality; wider range of products
2. A measure of the sales of one business as a percentage of total market sales
3. One firm dominates the market; it has a high market share
4. Any one from: it may push up prices; it may reduce quality in a protected market; it may not innovate
5. Any one from: it may use abnormal profits to invest in research and development and innovate; it may encourage other firms to be more innovative to remove the monopoly

Exam-style practice questions

1. B   **[1 mark]**
2. C   **[1 mark]**
3. D   **[1 mark]**
4. A   **[1 mark]**
5. D   **[1 mark]**
6. A   **[1 mark]**
7. a) Market share measures the sales of one business **[1]** as a percentage of the total market sales **[1]**.   **[2 marks]**
   b) A monopoly is a seller that dominates a market **[1]**; it has a high market share **[1]** (note: a pure monopoly is a single seller in a market)   **[2 marks]**
   c) Google was accused of abusing its market power **[1]** because consumers did not have real choice **[1]** when they were searching for items; Google allegedly misled them **[1]** so this was not in the public interest **[1]**.   **[4 marks]**
   d) Your answer should calculate $2.7 billion as a percentage of $ 89 billion, i.e. $\frac{2.7}{89} \times 100$ **[1]**; = 3.03% **[1]**   **[2 marks]**
   e) Explanations which might include:
      - becoming a monopoly may mean the business can become a price maker **[1]** and charge more **[1]**
      - becoming a monopoly may mean the business can earn higher (abnormal) profits **[1]** exploiting consumers **[1]**
      - becoming a monopoly may mean there is less competitive pressure **[1]** to innovate or improve customer service **[1]**.   **[4 marks]**
   f) Coherent analysis which might include:
      - highly innovative **[1]** creating products others cannot imitate **[1]**
      - buy up competitors **[1]** removing rivals **[1]**
      - strong brand loyalty **[1]** making it difficult for rivals to win customers **[1]**.   **[4 marks]**
   g) Award up to 4 marks for logical reasons why taxing monopolies may be desirable, e.g taxing these profits generates revenue for the government, which can be used for other purposes to benefit society; taxes may help to reduce behaviours / external costs that are against the public interest.
   Award up to 4 marks for logical reasons why alternative ways of controlling behavior may be desirable, e.g. legislation or government taking control of business.   **[6 marks]**
   h) Award up to 4 marks for logical reasons why a monopoly may be bad for consumers, e.g. using market power to push up price and potentially reduce quality.
   Award up to 4 marks for logical reasons why a monopoly may be good for consumers, e.g. using abnormal profits to invest in research and development; abnormal profits may act as incentive to others to innovate to gain abnormal profits.   **[6 marks]**
8. a) This is the service sector **[1]**, e.g tourism, education and finance **[1]**.   **[2 marks]**
   b) Explanations which might include:
   size of a business can be measured in different ways such as sales **[1]**, i.e the value of what has been sold **[1]**, assets **[1]**, i.e the value of what it owns **[1]**, number of employees **[1]**, i.e the total number of people who work for it **[1]**.   **[4 marks]**
   c) Coherent analysis which might include:
   Small businesses
      - can bring jobs **[1]** reducing unemployment in the economy **[1]**
      - can bring new products **[1]** creating more choice for consumers **[1]**
      - can innovate **[1]** leading to more choice and greater efficiency **[1]**
      - can provide greater competition for larger firms **[1]** leading to more innovation or lower prices **[1]**.   **[6 marks]**
   d) **Explain what internal economies of scale are,** e.g. technical, bulk buying, financial.
   Explain that a business might experience internal diseconomies of scale, e.g. due to problems with control, coordination and communication.   **[8 marks]**
9. a) Answers may include: nature of the job **[1]**, e.g. whether it is interesting and has variety **[1]**, non-monetary characteristics **[1]**, e.g. working hours and conditions **[1]**.   **[2 marks]**
   b) Explanations which might include:
      - the minimum wage is the minimum wage rate that all employees must earn in the country **[1]**
      - this has an impact if employees would otherwise earn less than this in the free market **[1]**; it will increase earnings **[1]**
      - however, at the BBC most employees will earn more than this anyway **[1]**
      - although they may feel their pay is low, it is higher than the minimum by law so minimum wage would not have an effect **[1]**.   **[4 marks]**
   c) Coherent analysis which might include:
      - how much the output can be sold for **[1]** – the more it is sold for the greater demand will be **[1]** and higher the wage **[1]**
      - how productive the employee is **[1]**; the more productive they are the more output they produce and the more they will be paid **[1]**
      - training period **[1]**; the longer the training period the lower the supply **[1]** and the higher the equilibrium wage **[1]**
      - the skills required **[1]**; the more skills needed the lower the supply **[1]** and the higher the equilibrium wage **[1]**.   **[6 marks]**
   d) **Explain the benefits of trade union membership,** e.g. greater protection from exploitation and better working conditions.
   Explain the potential disadvantages of membership, e.g. the costs of being a member, may lose the ability to bargain individually.   **[8 marks]**

4 Government and macro economy

The role and macroeconomic aims of government
1. The income of the economy increases
2. To increase the income of its country and the income per person
3. Because unemployment is a waste of resources and is inefficient
4. It measures the value of a country's transactions with the rest of the world
5. The organisations that are owned and run by the government

Fiscal policy
1. The use of government spending and taxation policies to influence the economy
2. Progressive
3. Direct tax is paid directly from earnings or profits; indirect tax is paid when a product is bought
4. Government spending is greater than taxation revenue
5. Any three from: defence; healthcare; education; transport; justice

Monetary policy

1. Attempts to control money supply and interest rates to influence the economy
2. The cost of borrowing money and the reward for savings
3. It might encourage borrowing by firms for investment
4. It might encourage borrowing by households (as it is cheaper to borrow) and, therefore, increase consumption
5. It might encourage foreign investors to want to save in the country; is likely to increase demand for currency and increase the exchange rate

Supply-side policy

1. Policies designed to increase aggregate supply in the economy
2. Any two from: lower tax rates to encourage work; lower unemployment benefits; more training; providing information about jobs available; assisting with relocation; improving healthcare; changing legislation around trade union power
3. Increased investment by the government, e.g. into transport and communications
4. Any one from: investment in targeted industries; incentives to encourage investment and innovation; protecting infant industries; encouraging greater competition (limiting takeovers and mergers); encouraging startups (reducing bureaucracy involved)
5. Any one from: changing regulations to make it easier for financial organisation to set up; encouraging customers to search for the best deal to encourage efficiency

Economic growth

1. Gross domestic product; a measure of national income
2. GDP adjusted for the effects of inflation to show the purchasing power of national income
3. Negative GDP growth for two successive quarters of the year (i.e. 6 months)
4. Any two from: investment in infrastructure; incentives for investment and innovation; lower interest rates to encourage investment and spending; supply-side policies
5. An outward shift of the PPC

Employment and unemployment

1. Any two from: can cause poverty; can lead to social divisions / unrest; possible increase in time; wasted resources / inefficient economy
2. Individuals are unemployed because the industry they worked in is no longer competitive and they do not have the skills for other jobs
3. Increasing aggregate demand to create jobs
4. Any one from: training; provide more information; help employees relocate
5. The level of unemployment measures the number of people who are willing and able to work but are not employed at the given wage rate at a given moment in time; the unemployment rate is the number of people unemployed as a percentage of the total workforce

Inflation and deflation

1. A sustained increase in the general price level
2. Inflation caused by excess demand
3. Inflation caused by higher costs being passed on
4. Any two from: increase costs of inputs and, therefore, increase prices; uncertainty about economic conditions and, therefore, less investment; changes to menu costs; changes to shoe leather costs
5. May increase uncertainty and reduce investment

Exam-style practice questions

1. C [1 mark]
2. D [1 mark]
3. C [1 mark]
4. D [1 mark]
5. D [1 mark]
6. B [1 mark]

7. a) Gross domestic product is a measure of the value of income generated over a given time within a region [1]; it is a measure of national income [1]. [2 marks]
   b) Government spending exceeds its revenue [1]; over a period, typically a year [1]. [2 marks]
   c) The rate of tax paid increases [1] as income increases [1]. [2 marks]
   d) Explanations which might include:
      - that a deficit may be because of high levels of government spending [1], e.g. on education or defence [1] and / or low levels of tax revenue [1], e.g. low tax revenue [1]. [4 marks]
   e) Explanations which might include:
      - high unemployment [1] so some have low incomes [1]
      - lack of training and skills [1] so some have poorly paid jobs [1]
      - discrimination [1] so some are paid too little [1]. [4 marks]
   f) Explanations which might include:
      - higher fuel duties will increase the price [1] and this may discourage consumption [1]
      - fuel consumption can have external costs [1] so reducing the consumption may lead to a more efficient allocation of resources [1]
      - the demand for fuel is likely to be price inelastic [1] and so, by taxing this, the quantity demanded will fall less than the price increase (proportionately), which should lead to relatively large tax revenues for the government [1]. [4 marks]
   g) Award up to 4 marks for logical analysis of the possible private consequences of unemployment for those who are unemployed.
      Award up to 4 marks for logical analysis of the possible consequences for society as a whole in South Africa. [6 marks]
   h) Award up to 4 marks for logical reasons why supply-side policies might be a good way of increasing economic growth, e.g. supply-side policies.
      Award up to 4 marks for logical reasons why supply-side policies might not be a good way of increasing economic growth, e.g. depends on what policies they are, how they are implemented. [6 marks]

8. a) The maximum output an economy can produce [1] given its existing resources [1]. [2 marks]
   b) Explanations which might include:
      - lower incomes [1] because of not earning from work [1]
      - less spending [1] due to lower incomes [1]
      - possible social problems [1] due to frustration and lack of money [1]. [4 marks]
   c) Coherent analysis which might include:
      - cyclical (demand deficient) [1] due to lack of demand [1] leading to less need for employees [1]
      - frictional [1] due to people being between jobs [1] so waiting for next job [1]
      - seasonal [1] due to seasonal patterns of demand [1] e.g. fruit farming [1]
      - structural [1] due to changes in the competitiveness of industries [1], e.g. decline of an industry as costs too high relative to competitors abroad [1]. [6 marks]
   d) **Explain how boosting demand may reduce unemployment,** e.g lower taxes and / or more spending boosting demand creating jobs. Explain how this is suitable for cyclical unemployment.
      Explain other ways of reducing unemployment, e.g. by boosting the demand in the economy (through fiscal and monetary policies) or providing information and training. The method used by the government should be linked to the cause of unemployment. [8 marks]

9. a) A budget deficit occurs when the revenue of the government is less than its spending [1] over a given period [1]. **[2 marks]**
   b) Explanations which might include:
      • training increases productivity [1]
      • providing more information [1] so more people are aware of the jobs available and can find jobs more easily [1]
      • increasing the incentive to work [1] so more people can work and produce [1]. **[4 marks]**
   c) Coherent analysis which might include:
      • explain what is meant by fiscal policy [1]
      • explain how changes in government spending and taxation and benefit rates can affect unemployment [1]
      • explain the impact on, e.g. demand deficient unemployment [1]. For example, more government spending can increase demand for goods and services [1], creating more demand for employees [1], and reducing unemployment [1]. **[6 marks]**
   d) **Explain how an increase in government spending can reduce unemployment,** e.g. more spending can increase demand for goods and services, creating jobs and reducing unemployment.
      Explain how reducing taxes can reduce unemployment, e.g. reducing income tax or corporation tax can increase income and profits and increase demand, reducing unemployment; reducing income tax can increase the rewards from working, creating an incentive to work. **[8 marks]**

5 Economic development

Living standards
1. National income per person adjusted for inflation
2. How the income in the country is divided between its population
3. Any two from: does not necessarily reflect the quality of goods and services; does not show how income is distributed; does not include income from non-marketed output (e.g. barter) and unpaid work; does not reflect quality of life (e.g. how many hours are worked); does not include trade in the 'shadow economy'
4. Standard of living measures the income per person; cost of living measures the price level in the economy
5. Any one from: by using supply-side policies to boost economic growth / the capacity of the economy; by using demand-side policies to increase demand, potentially leading to higher output and income; monetary and fiscal policies can increase income more than population increases, leading to an increase in income per person

Poverty
1. When incomes fall significantly below what is required to live a modest but adequate existence
2. When individual or household income falls below some national average or median income
3. Any two from: unemployment; homelessness; low pay; addiction
4. Any two from: loss of status and self-respect; health issues; social exclusion / tension
5. Any two from: increase in national minimum wage; create more jobs; changes to taxation system; changes to benefits system; investment in education and healthcare; investment in training people; encouraging startup businesses / business growth; subsidies for certain services

Population
1. The median age of the population is increasing
2. The difference between the number of people entering and leaving the population of a country over a given period
3. Any one from: healthcare; education; social provisions, e.g. social care and clean water; environmental factors, e.g. natural disasters and pollution
4. Any one from: easing of regulations, e.g. relaxing visa requirements; a higher perceived quality of life / standard of living
5. Any one from: higher taxes on those in work to provide for those not working; higher healthcare bills

Differences in economic development between countries
1. A developing economy has a low income per person; but is growing fast
2. True
3. True
4. True
5. By allowing trade so the developing economy can export more; with more exports the businesses in the developing economy can earn more and pay employees more; this can lead to further spending and demand in the economy

Exam-style practice questions
1. D **[1 mark]**
2. D **[1 mark]**
3. C **[1 mark]**
4. C **[1 mark]**
5. A **[1 mark]**
6. a) A developing economy has a low income per person [1] but is growing fast [1]. **[2 marks]**
   b) The tertiary sector involves the provision of services [1]; e.g. education, healthcare and accounting [1]. **[2 marks]**
   c) Per capita income is the total income of a country divided by population [1]; it shows the average income per person [1]. **[2 marks]**
   d) Explanations which might include:
      • a large proportion of the population have low literacy [1], e.g. this is likely to reduce productivity [1]
      • still being an agricultural economy [1], e.g. dependent on products that are vulnerable to the weather, which can cause major shifts in supply and prices and incomes; reliant on imports of manufactured goods [1]. **[4 marks]**
   e) Explanations which might include:
      • economic growth leads to higher incomes [1]
      • higher incomes can lead to a better standard of living for Ethiopian citizens [1]
      • a higher standard of living reduces poverty [1] and makes the government popular [1]. **[4 marks]**
   f) Explanations which might include:
      • foreign firms might be attracted by low costs of factors of production in Ethiopia [1] because this can increase profits [1] and availability of labour in Ethiopia [1] which reduces costs [1]
      • might be attracted by government policies [1], e.g grants for locating there [1]
      • that the location (near seaports) is a good base for exporting to other parts of the world [1] reducing travel costs [1]. **[4 marks]**
   g) Award up to 4 marks for logical reasons why income per person is a good measure of development, i.e. it measures the standard of living.
      Award up to 4 marks for logical reasons why other measures might be better than income per person, e.g. education levels, the health of the population, birth rates and mortality rates. **[6 marks]**

h) Award up to 4 marks for logical reasons why greater trade can be good for the economy, e.g. open up export markets and lead to more earnings for the country; can mean more access to better and cheaper products for Ethiopian citizens; can allow Ethiopian businesses to access cheaper supplies.

Award up to 4 marks for logical reasons why greater trade might make it difficult for local businesses to grow (when facing international competitors). **[6 marks]**

7. a) This means that the percentage increase in national income each year **[1]** is relatively high **[1]**. **[2 marks]**
   b) Explanations which might include:
      • unemployment **[1]**; without a job, income falls **[1]**
      • low pay **[1]**, e.g. due to low skills **[1]**
      • illness **[1]**, preventing work **[1]**. **[4 marks]**
   c) Coherent analysis which might include:
      • increase the financial burden on the government **[1]**, e.g. more healthcare provision **[1]** which needs investment **[1]**
      • need to finance areas such as pensions and healthcare **[1]**; this may increase the tax burden on those in work **[1]** and this may reduce the incentive to work or make profits **[1]**
      • might affect consumption patterns **[1]**, e.g. less demand for toys **[1]** leading to different output by producers **[1]**. **[6 marks]**
   d) **Explain how a multinational might help reduce poverty,** e.g. by bringing investment, jobs and economic growth, which will create jobs within the multinational and also for suppliers of the business.
      Explain that the effect depends on the behaviour of the multinational, e.g. depends on level of investment, what jobs are offered, whether profits are reinvested into the country, whether local staff are employed and how many local suppliers there are. **[8 marks]**

8. a) GDP measures the national income of an economy over a period of time **[1]**. The Human Development Index includes GDP **[1]** but also considers health **[1]** and education **[1]**. **[2 marks]**
   b) Logical explanation may include:
      • higher birth rate leads to higher population **[1]** which can, over time, increase labour force **[1]**, which increases factors of production **[1]**
      • this can lead to an increase in output **[1]** and income in the economy **[1]**
      • in short run it may mean more people without an increase in output **[1]** as there are more children **[1]** so GDP per head falls **[1]**. **[4 marks]**
   c) Coherent analysis which might include:
      • how GDP measures income **[1]**
      • that the Human Development Index is a summary measure of average achievement of a number of important dimensions **[1]**, such as health, education and standard of living **[1]**
      • how these may change in different ways **[1]**, e.g. they may have more income **[1]** but this does not necessarily mean it is invested in education or health **[1]**
      • that it is possible to have high incomes but the HDI to be relatively lower **[1]** – HDI measures a wider range of measures than just income **[1]**. **[6 marks]**
   d) **Explain how the minimum wage might reduce poverty.** If the minimum wage is higher than the free market wage for low income earners it will raise their earnings and bring some out of poverty. However, it will mean fewer are employed, so the unemployed will be worse off.
      Explain other measures that may be used, such as efforts to get more people into work, e.g. more training and more information, and investment in education. **[8 marks]**

6 International trade and globalisation

International specialisation
1. When one country has a lower opportunity cost in the production of a good or service compared to another country
2. True
3. Any one from: better resources; better technology; skills and experience
4. More choice of goods at lower prices
5. Any one from: can import resources at a lower price than it can produce itself; can help keep costs down; can enable faster economic growth

Free trade and protection
1. Tariff
2. Quota
3. Infant industries
4. When one government introduces protectionist measures in response to another government using them
5. Any one from: increases prices; allows inefficient domestic producers to continue in production; less choice for consumers; a reduction in quality and customer service

Foreign exchange rates
1. The value of one currency in terms of another
2. Increase in demand for the currency, e.g. due to greater demand for the country's goods and services or higher interest rates
3. Appreciation
4. Any one from: fall in demand (e.g. less demand from abroad for its goods and services); an increase in supply (e.g. increased demand for imports)
5. An appreciation of a currency decreases the price of imports, all other factors unchanged

Current account of balance of payments
1. The sum of the balance of trade (goods and services exports less imports), primary income (net income from abroad) and secondary income (net current transfers)
2. The value of money leaving the country on the current account is the greater than the value of money entering the country
3. Lack of international competitiveness; strong value of the currency
4. Likely to reduce demand, reduce income, increase unemployment, reduces inflation
5. By reducing the value of its currency – this can make exports cheaper in foreign currency and imports more expensive domestically, reducing the deficit

Exam-style practice questions
1. D **[1 mark]**
2. B **[1 mark]**
3. B **[1 mark]**
4. C **[1 mark]**
5. a) Deficit **[1 mark]**
   b) The economic and political union between member European countries **[1]**; within the EU there is freedom of movement of people, goods, services and money / there are common tariffs against imports from non-member countries **[1]**. **[2 marks]**
   c) No barriers to trade between countries **[1]**; e.g. no tariffs or quotas **[1]**. **[2 marks]**
   d) Answers may include:
      • favourable trade agreements **[1]** and trading conditions **[1]**
      • Japanese consumers have strong preferences for EU products **[1]**
      • favourable exchange rates **[1]**. **[4 marks]**

e) Logical explanation which might include:
Businesses will need time to prepare for the new trading conditions [1], e.g. European producers must have time to ensure they can compete with producers from Japan [1]; the change may cause some businesses to close and lead to unemployment in some regions [1]; governments will want to give businesses times to prepare for this to reduce impact on industries [1]. **[4 marks]**

f) Average income = $\dfrac{\text{total income}}{\text{number of people}}$

$= \dfrac{\$4\,932\,000\,000\,000}{127\,000\,000}$ [1]

$= \$38\,834.64$ [1] **[2 marks]**

g) Logical explanation might include:
- the benefits of trade [1], e.g. can benefit from the skills and resources of other countries [1]
- that they may be different brands and models [1]; trade gives consumers more choice [1]. **[4 marks]**

h) Logical explanation might include:
- may be due to supply increasing [1]
- more supply might push prices down [1]
- that it may be due to the power of the buyers, e.g. the big supermarkets [1] – they can force the price down [1] as they are in a strong bargaining position [1]. **[5 marks]**

i) Award up to 4 marks for logical reasons explaining impact may be desirable for some groups, e.g lower prices and more choice for consumers.
Award up to 4 marks for logical reasons explaining impact may not be desirable for some groups, e.g some producers may face more competition. **[6 marks]**

6. a) The value of money leaving the country on the current account over a given time period [1] is greater than the value of money entering the country [1]. **[2 marks]**

b) Logical explanation which might include
- tariffs [1] which involve placing a tax on foreign goods and services making them less competitive [1]
- quotas [1] which involves a limit on the number of foreign goods or services [1]. **[4 marks]**

c) Your answer should:
- Coherent analysis which might include:
Earnings from goods and services exported may be less than spending on imports [1] due to lack of competitiveness [1] such as higher costs [1] or lack of productivity [1] or poor quality [1] or strong exchange rate [1]. **[6 marks]**

d) **Explain why trade protection may be adopted,** e.g. to protect infant industry, retaliation, to protect strategic industries
Explain the benefits of free trade, e.g. more choice of goods and services for consumers at lower prices, economic growth, consumption outside of the PPC. **[8 marks]**

7. a) The price of one currency in terms of another [1], e.g. $1 = £0.80 [1] **[2 marks]**

b) Explanations which might include:
- uncompetitive prices [1] making local goods more appealing [1]
- poor quality [1] reducing demand [1]
- high income domestically [1] leads to more imports [1]. **[4 marks]**

c) Coherent analysis which might include:
- protectionism may reduce quantity of goods available to consumers [1], e.g. through quotas [1] reducing their choice [1]
- protectionism may increase prices [1], e.g through tariffs [1] and increase prices for consumers
- may make foreign inputs more expensive for businesses [1], e.g. with cost of tariff [1] increasing costs [1] and reducing profits [1]
- tariffs may raise revenue for the government [1] giving more funds for investment elsewhere [1]
- may create or protect jobs in protected industries [1] which may win votes [1] but overall there may be fewer jobs in the economy [1]. **[6 marks]**

d) **Explain how a fall in the exchange rate is likely to reduce imports and increase exports,** e.g. due to higher export prices abroad and more expensive import prices in local currency, improving the current account deficit.
Explain how this may change over time, e.g. as demand for exports and imports becomes more price sensitive and consumers change their behaviours. **[8 marks]**

Glossary

Absolute advantage – when a country can produce products at a lower cost than a competitor

Absolute poverty – severe deprivation of basic human needs, including food, safe drinking water, sanitation facilities, health, shelter, education and information

Ageing population – when the median age of a population increases, e.g. due to a decline in birth rates or an increase in life expectancy

Aggregate demand – the total demand for goods and services in an economy

Aggregate supply – the total supply of goods and services in an economy

Appreciation – an increase in value

Average cost (AC) – unit cost; total cost divided by output

Average revenue (AR) – a measure of the amount paid by customers per item; the price of a product

Backward vertical integration – a firm joins with another firm at an earlier stage of the same production process, e.g. a car manufacturer joins with a tyre manufacturer

Balance of payments – a record of all of a country's financial transactions with the rest of the world over a year

Balance of trade – the difference between the values of exports (money coming into the country from sales abroad) and imports (money leaving the country for purchase abroad)

Barter – the exchange of goods or services for others goods or services (without using money)

Basic economic problem – there are limited resources and unlimited human wants, so decisions have to be made about what is produced, how it is produced and who it is produced for

Birth rate – usually measured by the number of live births per thousand people in the population per year

Boom – occurs when output is growing faster than the average trend rate

Budget – measures the difference between government spending and revenue over a given period

Budget deficit – government spending is greater than taxation revenue

Budget position – the difference between government spending and government revenue in a given period, usually a year

Budget surplus – government spending is less than its revenue

Buffer stock – stock bought by the government when there is excess supply and sold when there is excess demand to help stabilise prices in volatile markets

Capital – financial and material wealth; goods used to produce other goods, e.g. equipment and technology

Capital goods – goods, such as machines and equipment, which are an investment for the future

Central bank – manages a country's currency, money supply and interest rates on behalf of the government

Claimant count – the number of people entitled to claim benefits over a given time period

Command (or planned) economy – an economy in which the basic economic questions are solved by the government allocating resources

Commercial bank – high street banks; banks that accept deposits, lend to households and firms and provide an efficient means of payment

Comparative advantage – when one country can produce a good or service at a lower opportunity cost than another

Complement – a good that is closely linked to another good, e.g. a printer and printer cartridges, so the demand for and price of one product has a direct effect on the demand for and price of the other

Conglomerate integration – when a firm acquires an unrelated business, e.g. a car manufacturer acquires a hotel business

Consumer – households or individuals; the end-users of products

Consumer Price Index (CPI) – a weighted index that measures changes in the price of consumer goods and services purchased by households

Consumption – to consume; the amount of an individual or household's income spent on goods and services

Consumption goods – goods for immediate consumption, e.g. food

Contraction – a decrease in quantity demanded due to a price rise / a decrease in supply due to a fall in price

Cooperative – organisations that are jointly owned

Cost of living – the amount of money needed to sustain a certain level of living for a household, including basic expenses such as accommodation, food and clothing

Cost-push inflation – a rise in prices due to an increase in costs

Death rate – usually measured by the number of deaths per thousand people in the population per year

Deficit – occurs when expenses (outgoings) are higher than income

Deflation – a sustained fall in the general price level over a given period

Demand – the quantity of goods and services that buyers are willing and able to buy

Demand curve – a graph showing the quantity that buyers are willing and able to buy at each and every price, all other factors unchanged

Demand-pull inflation – a rise in price caused by an increase in aggregate demand

Demerit goods – goods that are worse for the individual that the individual may appreciate, e.g. cigarettes and drugs

Dependency ratio – the percentage of dependants in an economy compared to the number of people of working age

Depreciation – a fall in value

Depression – occurs when there is a fall in real GDP of more than 10% from the peak of the economic cycle to its lowest point of recession

Derived demand – demand for a factor of production that occurs as a result of the demand for a product or service

Direct tax – a tax taken directly from earnings, e.g. income tax and corporation tax

Disequilibrium – at the given price, the quantity demanded is greater than the quantity supplied (there is a shortage) or the quantity supplied is greater than the quantity demanded (excess supply)

Dissave – to spend a greater amount of money than available income, e.g. by using savings or a pension fund

Economic agents – the different groups within an economy, e.g. consumers, employees, producers and government

Economic (business or trade) cycle – the growth pattern of an economy's income over time, including boom, recession, slump and recovery

Economic goods – a good that can only be produced if resources are moved from the production of another good, i.e. production involves an opportunity cost

Economic growth – a shift outwards in the PPC; the total amount of goods and services that the economy can produce increases

Embargo – a ban on trade in particular goods and services with another country

Employee – someone in work; someone employed by another economic agent

Employment – the number of people in work

Enterprise – refers to the management expertise needed to think of new products and processes and combine resources to set up a new project or business

Entrepreneur – someone who comes up with new ideas and takes the risk to develop new business opportunities

Equilibrium – quantity supplied equals quantity demanded at a given price

Exchange rate – the price of one currency in terms of another

Export subsidy – a direct payment, low-cost loan or tax relief for exporters from the government to encourage export of goods

Exports – goods and services sold abroad

Extension – an increase in the quantity demanded due to a fall in price / an increase in supply due to a rise in price

External economies of scale – when unit costs decrease at every level of output due to factors outside of the business itself

Factor mobility – refers to how easily factors can move from one business or industry to another

Factors of production – the inputs into the production process: land, labour, capital and enterprise

Fertility rate – the average number of children a woman will give birth to over her lifetime

Financial intermediary – an organisation that provides a link between savers and borrowers, e.g. banks, building societies, pension funds and insurance companies

Finite resources – resources that are limited and will eventually run out

Firm – a business organisation; a business or company

Fiscal drag – occurs when an increase in income means that higher taxes have to be paid, so the individual is no better off in real terms

Fiscal policy – the means by which a government adjusts its spending levels and tax rates to monitor and influence a nation's economy

Fixed cost (FC) – a cost that does not change with output, e.g. rent or interest on a loan

Fixed (or managed) exchange rate – an exchange rate that is kept at a particular level by the government

Fixed-rate loan – a loan for which interest repayments are agreed at the start (are fixed)

Floating exchange rate – when the price of a currency is determined by market forces, i.e. by the supply and demand of the currency in the foreign currency markets

Foreign exchange rate – the price of one currency in terms of another

Forward vertical integration – when a business joins with another at a stage nearer the customer, e.g. a manufacturer buys a retailer

Free goods – goods that do not involve an opportunity cost

Free market economy – an economy in which the basic economic problem is solved by the decisions of firms and households in the private sector

Free rider problem – when people use a public resource or good without paying their share of the cost

Free trade – unrestricted trade (occurs when there are no barriers to trade)

Geographical immobility – employees cannot move to or work in another region, e.g. due to prohibitive housing prices / transport costs

Globalisation – integration of economies, industries, societies and cultures around the world

Government – the means by which state policy is enforced

Gross domestic product (GDP) – a measure of the income earned in an economy over a year, i.e. the value of the output of final goods and services produced in a year

Gross national income (GNI) – gross domestic product, plus incomes earned by foreign residents, minus income earned in the domestic economy by non-residents

Horizontal integration – when a business joins with another at the same stage of the same process, e.g. one bank joins with another bank

Household – includes all the persons living together in one housing unit, e.g. a house or apartment

Human Development Index (HDI) – a measure of economic development and social welfare, based on life expectancy, education and standard of living

Imports – goods and services sold to people within a country that are produced abroad

Incidence of the tax burden – the division of the tax burden between the consumers and the producers

Income – how much is earned over a given period; a flow of earnings

Income distribution – refers to the way in which the total income of a country is distributed amongst its population

Income inequality – when income is distributed unevenly, so that some individuals / households have significantly more than others

Increasing returns – when output increases more than the proportional increase in inputs

Indirect tax – a charge on products that is payable by producers to the government; it may be a specific per unit tax or an *ad valorem* tax

Individual demand curve – shows the quantity an individual consumer is willing and able to buy at each price, all other factors unchanged

Individual supply curve – shows the quantity an individual producer is willing and able to produce at each price and every price, all other factors unchanged

Inflation – a sustained increase in the general price level over a period of time

Interest rate – the cost of borrowing money and the reward for saving

Internal diseconomies of scale – a rise in costs that occurs when the scale of production increases

Internal economies of scale – a fall in costs that occurs when the scale of production increases

International trade – when countries buy and sell goods and services from each other

Joint demand – when two products are always brought together, so demand is the same

Labour – the human input into production; refers to the size and skills of the workforce

Labour immobility – when it is difficult for labour to move from one business or industry to another, e.g. due to a difference in skills or difficulty moving to a different area

Land – a factor of production; includes land and natural resources, such as oil

Level of unemployment – the number of people who are willing and able to work but are not employed at the given wage rate at a given moment in time

Loan – a fixed amount that is borrowed and repaid at agreed rates

Macroeconomics – a study of the economy as a whole

Market – made up of supply and demand; occurs when buyers and sellers come together to trade (exchange goods and services)

Market demand curve – constructed by adding together the quantity demanded by all the different consumers at each and every price, all other factors unchanged

Market disequilibrium – this occurs when the quantity demanded does not equal the quantity supplied

Market economic system – this occurs when resources are allocated by market forces of supply and demand

Market equilibrium – this occurs when the quantity supplied equals the quantity demanded and there is no incentive to change

Market failure – occurs in a free market when the outcome of the market is not satisfactory from a social point of view

Market share – a company's sales as a percentage of the total sales in the industry

Market supply curve – constructed by adding together the quantity supplied by all the different producers supply at each price and every price

Maximum price – set by the government to limit the price that can be charged in a market

Menu costs – the costs incurred by a firm in order to change their prices

Merger – when two or more businesses join together to create a new business

Merit goods – goods that are better for the individual than the individual may appreciate, e.g. education

Microeconomics – the study of specific markets within an economy

Minimum price – set by the government to limit how low the price can go in a market

Mixed economy – an economy with a private sector and a public sector

Monetary policy – the central bank's actions to influence interest rates, the supply of money and the exchange rate to affect the economy

Monopoly – occurs when there is a single seller in a market

Monopoly power – occurs when one business dominates the industry and has power over others

Mortgage – a loan obtained to pay for property

Movement along a demand curve – a change in the quantity demanded due to a change in price

Movement along a supply curve – a change in the quantity supplied due to a change in price

Multinational company (MNC) – a company that has bases in more than one country

Nationalisation – when assets are transferred from the private sector to the public sector

Net emigration – the number of people leaving a country exceeds the number entering over that period

Net immigration – the number of people entering a country exceeds the number leaving over that period

Net migration – the difference between the number of people coming into a country and the number leaving a country over a given period

Non-diminishable – refers to a free good; if someone consumes a product, it does not reduce the amount available for others

Non-excludable – refers to a free good; non-paying consumers cannot be prevented from accessing it

Normal goods – goods for which demand increases as income increases

Objectives – these are targets, e.g. to increase profits

Occupational immobility – employees cannot move from one industry to another due to a lack of skills

Opportunity cost – the alternative that is given up / sacrificed when a decision is made about resource allocation, e.g. if resources are allocated to produce more computer games they cannot also be used for healthcare

Optimum population – the theoretical population size at which, working with all available resources, there would be the highest standard of living for all people in the country

Overall poverty – insufficient income and resources to allow citizens a sustainable livelihood, characterised by hunger, ill health, limited access to education, unsatisfactory housing and social discrimination

Overdraft – a facility to borrow up to a certain amount from a bank and only pay interest on the amount actually borrowed

Overpopulation – when there are too many people in a country given the resources available

Partnership – a type of business organisation; two or more people working together in the pursuit of profit

Pattern of employment – refers to the types of job that people within an economy do

Population – the total number of people in a country at a given moment

Population structure – the way in which the population is divided up between males and females of different age groups

Price elastic – a percentage change in price leads to a more than proportionate change in another factor

Price elasticity of demand (PED) – the percentage change in quantity demanded in relation to percentage change in price, all other factors unchanged

Price elasticity of supply (PES) – the percentage change in quantity supplied in response to a percentage change in price

Price inelastic – a percentage change in price leads to a less than proportionate change (less than 1) in another factor

Price mechanism – the process whereby the price adjusts to bring about equilibrium

Primary income – income earned by a country's citizens who own assets overseas, including earnings, profits, dividends on investments abroad and interest

Primary market (stock exchange) – where bonds and shares are sold for the first time

Primary sector – made up of the farming and extractive industries, such as oil and coal

Private limited company (ltd) – a company owned by shareholders; shareholders have limited liability; the shares cannot be advertised

Private sector – made up of businesses owned by private individuals

Privatisation – when assets are transferred from the public sector to the private sector

Producer – any business or firm that produces a good or service

Production – the total output of a business

Production possibility curve (PPC) – shows the maximum combination of goods and services that an economy can produce with its factors of production at a given moment

Productive efficiency – all resources are being fully utilised; more of one product can only be produced if less of another is produced

Productive inefficiency – when an economy is operating inside the PPF, i.e. more of one product can be produced without producing less of another (resources are available)

Productivity – a measure of the output in relation to the inputs used to produce it

Profit – the difference between revenue and costs

Profit maximisation – when a business earns the highest possible profit achievable

Protection (protectionist measures) – barriers to trade; measures to protect one country's producers from foreign competition

Public corporation – organisations that are state owned, such as schools and hospitals

Public goods – goods that are non-diminishable and non-excludable

Public limited company (plc) – a company owned by shareholders; shareholders have limited liability; shares can be sold to the general public

Public sector – made up of organisations that are owned by the government

Quota – a limit placed on the quantity of a good or service allowed into a country

Real GDP per head (or per capita) – the value of gross domestic product (GDP) adjusted for inflation and divided by the population size to give a value per person

Real national income per person – the value of gross national income (GNI) adjusted for inflation and divided by the population size to give a value per person

Recession – a fall in national income (GDP) for two consecutive quarters (i.e. six months) or more

Recovery – when real GDP picks up from the low point of the recession

Regulation – rules made by a government or other authority to control the way in which something is done

Relative poverty – when individual or household income falls below the national average or median income

Renewable – resources that can be replaced / come from a sustainable source

Resources – inputs used to produce goods or services; the factors of production

Revenue – the income of the business; equal to the spending (or expenditure) of consumers; price per unit × number of units sold

Savings – money from income that is not spent (is saved)

Secondary income – involves money transfers between central governments and grants

Secondary market (stock exchange) – the trade of second-hand shares

Secondary sector – made up of the firms that take raw materials and process them, e.g. manufacturing

Shareholder – an individual or firm that owns at least one share in another company

Shift in demand – more or less is demanded at each and every price

Shift in supply – more or less is supplied at each and every price

Shoe leather costs – refers to the opportunity cost of time and energy that a firm puts into trying to counteract the effects of inflation

Shortage – the quantity demanded is greater than the quantity supplied

Slowdown – when the rate of income growth slows down, but the economy is still growing

Slump – a sustained and major recession leading to a significant fall in output

Social benefits – the total benefits to society of producing a good or service, i.e. the private plus the external benefits

Social costs – the costs to society of producing a good or service, e.g. pollution and / or congestion

Sole trader – a business set up by an individual (the individual is the business); the business has unlimited liability

Specialisation (international trade) – when a country or region specialises in producing the product where it has a comparative advantage

Specialisation (labour market) – occurs when jobs are divided into smaller tasks and employees are trained to do one of these specific tasks

Standard of living – usually measured by real GDP per head or real national income per capita; refers to the level of comfort and wealth available to a household or socioeconomic group

Stock exchange – a market for shares

Strike – when employees withdraw their labour in protest / to force a decision from their employer

Subsidy – a benefit, usually a cash payment or tax reduction, given to a firm by the government to help remove some type of burden

Substitute – a similar product, which may replace another if market conditions change

Supply – the quantity that producers are willing and able to produce at each and every price, all other factors unchanged

Supply curve – this shows the quantity that producers are willing and able to produce at each and every price, all other factors unchanged

Supply-side policy – a government policy with the aim of increasing productivity and shifting aggregate supply to the right

Surplus – the quantity supplied is greater than the quantity demanded

Takeover – when a business gains control of another, e.g. by buying the majority of its shares

Tariff – taxes on foreign goods and services and increases to their price

Taxation – charges imposed on households and firms to raise revenue for government spending

Tertiary sector – made up of firms that provide services, e.g. education and banking

Total cost (TC) – fixed costs plus variable costs

Total revenue (TR) – the total expenditure by consumers; the total income of a business; calculated by price multiplied by quantity

Trade union – an organisation that represents employees and works to protect their rights

Underpopulation – when there are too few people in an area to use the resources effectively, given the level of technology

Unemployment rate – the number of people unemployed as a percentage of the total workforce

Variable costs (VC) – costs that change with output, e.g. the costs of materials

Variable-rate loan – a loan for which the interest repayments vary as interest rates in the economy change

Wealth – a stock concept; the stock of assets (e.g. shares and property) a person, business or economy has at a given moment in time

Weighted price index – a list of prices that are weighted to reflect the relative importance of the different goods and services, e.g. essential foodstuffs and services have a higher weighting than luxury goods

Work to rule – when employees do exactly what is in their contract and no more

Cover photo © photowind / Shutterstock

p.15 – Fig. 1 & 2: data © World Bank / OECD; p.15 – Fig. 3: data © MOTIE;
p.44 – Fig. 1 & 2: data © OECD; p.88 – Fig. 1: data © Stats SA;
p.101 – Fig. 1: data © World Bank / OECD; p.117 – Fig. 2: data © European Union, 1995–2017

Published by Letts Educational
An imprint of HarperCollins*Publishers*
The News Building
1 London Bridge Street
London
SE1 9GF

ISBN 978-0-00-826013-2

First published 2018

10 9 8 7 6 5 4 3 2 1

© HarperCollins*Publishers* Limited 2018

Commissioned by Gillian Bowman
Project managed by Rachel Allegro
Edited by Rebecca Skinner
Proofread by Louise Robb
Cover design by Paul Oates
Typesetting by QBS
Production by Natalia Rebow and Lyndsey Rogers
Printed and bound in the UK by Martins the Printers

MIX
Paper from
responsible sources
FSC™ C007454

This book is produced from independently certified FSC paper
to ensure responsible forest management.

For more information visit: www.harpercollins.co.uk/green

Notes